AUDACIOUS
MISSIONS OF WORLD WAR II

THE
NATIONAL
ARCHIVES

OSPREY
PUBLISHING

AUDACIOUS
MISSIONS OF WORLD WAR II

The National Archives

OSPREY PUBLISHING
Bloomsbury Publishing Plc
PO Box 883, Oxford, OX1 9PL, UK
1385 Broadway, 5th Floor, New York, NY 10018, USA

E-mail: info@ospreypublishing.com

www.ospreypublishing.com

OSPREY is a trademark of Osprey Publishing Ltd
First published in Great Britain in 2020

A catalogue record for this book is available from the British Library.

ISBN: HB 978-1-4728-2995-5; ePDF 978-1-4728-2994-8;
ePub 978-1-4728-2996-2; XML 978-1-4728-2997-9

20 21 22 23 24   10 9 8 7 6 5 4 3 2 1

Index by Zoe Ross
Printed and bound in India by Replika Press Private Ltd.
Page layout by Myriam Bell Design, Shrewsbury, UK

Front cover (top): Infantry of 11th Armoured Division advance near Eterville, Normandy, 29 June 1944.
The division went on to support the right flank of Operation *Market Garden*. (Sgt Laing/ Imperial War
Museums via Getty Images)
Front cover (bottom) and back cover: An RAF Lysander reconnaissance plane, 25 October 1941.
(Haywood Magee/Picture Post/Getty Images)

Osprey Publishing supports the Woodland Trust, the UK's leading woodland conservation charity.
To find out more about our authors and books visit **www.ospreypublishing.com**. Here you will find
extracts, author interviews, details of forthcoming events and the option to sign up for our newsletter.

CONTENTS

INTRODUCTION

World War II in Europe was fought over land, sea and air for six long years between 1939 and 1945, yet one way to look at the conflict is as a series of missions which influenced the ebb and flow of the war. In fact, the fighting was not always continuous and was sometimes unplanned during those years – the 'Phoney War' in 1939 surely demonstrates that – but comprised many different missions which were often meticulously organized and highly dangerous. It is these missions, as opposed to the overarching campaigns of the war, which are the subject of this book.

The National Archives at Kew holds fascinating files on the raids and missions described in this book. From well-known raids such as *Operation Chastise* – the 'Dam Busters' raid – to lesser known but perhaps no less significant ones such as *Anthropoid* – the assassination of high-ranking Nazi official Reinhard Heydrich – this is a compilation of just a few of the missions that took place during World War II. What they all had in common was intensive planning that went into the operations, and an element of danger. Indeed, some operations were considered so dangerous that they were never seriously put into practice, such as *Foxley* – the planned assassination of Hitler, which was permanently shelved in 1945 as the war came to an end. This British Special Operations Executive (SOE) mission was to involve a sniper attack on Hitler at his Berghof retreat; needless to say it was not a task from which the assassin was expected to return alive. More outlandish possibilities are outlined in the original files, such as a suggestion to poison the Führer's tea. The sheer personal risk and physical endurance required for many of these missions is evident from other examples, such as Operations *Grouse*, *Freshman*, *Swallow* and *Gunnerside*. This was the sabotage of Nazi 'heavy water' installations in Norway, carried out by SOE and the Norwegian resistance and later immortalized in the 1965 film *The Heroes of Telemark*.

The immense danger in wrecking Nazi plans for an atom bomb is borne out by the toll that the raid took; those captured by the Germans were executed.

The missions in this book were driven by high-level strategy, and could be said in some cases to have dictated the course of the war itself – although there is also ongoing debate about whether some of the raids met their actual objectives. Not all were considered to be unalloyed successes when compared with the original objectives, although many did achieve what they had set out to do. *Claymore*, a raid on Norway's Lofoten Islands in 1941, was a complete success with factories, Axis shipping and oil tanks destroyed. It was part of a series of raids on Norway during the war, which formed part of Churchill's strategy of keeping the Germans on high alert, with no knowledge of where the Allies would strike next. Operation *Catechism* came about after numerous attempts to sink the mighty German battleship *Tirpitz*; amongst these attempts was Operation *Source*, where the Royal Navy used mini-submarines to put *Tirpitz* out of action for six months. Nevertheless, the job had to be completed and in 1944 a huge air raid by the RAF finally sank *Tirpitz*. The famous raid on the Ruhr dams by the RAF's 617 Squadron came at a time in the war when Allied bombing raids on Germany were becoming much more frequent. Operation *Chastise* damaged or destroyed a number of dams in the Ruhr valley which were important for German industry and hydro-electricity, and in itself was a boost to morale back in Britain.

The planning that went into many of the missions was intense. *Jubilee*, which was the infamous raid on Dieppe in 1942 by Combined Operations, shows how incredibly detailed maps were produced to guide the mission. In *Biting* – the attempt to capture a German radar at Bruneval – the plans went further and a scale model of the site was devised, made out of rubber and depicting the terrain right down to every shrub, fencepost and rock. This level of planning gave those who participated in the raid the confidence of knowing what they were parachuting into. Some of the more bizarre preparations were carried out as part of *Mincemeat*, the now famous plan to deceive the German high command into thinking that the Allies' main military thrust in the Mediterranean as part of their 'second front' would be through the Balkans, rather than through Sicily. This involved full-scale deception and the forging of sensitive documents detailing the Allies' plans, which were placed on a genuine body procured from St Stephen's Hospital, Fulham, and deposited at sea for the Germans to find. The idea was that these documents would be passed up the German chain of command to Hitler, thus deceiving him as to the Allies' intentions. A bank overdraft and theatre tickets, as well as letters purporting to be to Gen Dwight D. Eisenhower, were convincingly used to this purpose.

The missions here are arranged according to the various wartime organizations which sponsored them. Combined Operations and SOE are perhaps best known for these, and a selection of their most famous operations are included in Part One and Part Two, beginning with the early raids of the war in Norway (*Claymore*, *Anklet and Archery*) and progressing through to *Biting*, *Chariot* and *Jubilee*. Similarly, Part Two begins with the earlier SOE missions such as *Anthropoid* and covers the progression of tactics and planning through to later missions such as *Gunnerside* and the abduction of Gen Kreipe by agents in Crete. The Royal Navy and the RAF were also responsible for missions, however, and it is again interesting to note how the planning changed as experience was gained during the course of the war. For example, there was more than one attempt to sink the *Tirpitz* and numerous tactics were trialled such as mini-submersibles in Operation *Source*. Eventually the RAF was brought in to sink the vessel through aerial bombing, and even then it took more than one attempt, with their objective finally achieved during Operation *Catechism*. The sinking of the *Bismarck*, by contrast, involved a sea and air operation with practically an entire fleet at the Royal Navy's disposal in order to locate and destroy the vessel. Operations *Market Garden*, *Chastise*, *Catechism* and *Crossbow* are four of the many missions in which the RAF was involved. Later in the war, as southern England came under attack from Hitler's V1 'flying bombs' and V2 rockets, it was the aerial bombing of Operation *Crossbow* which mitigated the damage and destruction and surely saved many lives in the process.

Many of the most significant wartime exploits of all time were planned and carried out during the Second World War. This is but a small selection, which demonstrates the incredible planning, risk and execution of those missions through the records that they left behind.

INTRODUCTION

The story of Combined Operations is long and complicated. This is a selective appraisal of some key raids in the years 1940–42.

On the last day of the Dunkirk evacuation, 4 June 1940, Prime Minister Winston Churchill wrote to his Principal Military Adviser, Maj Gen Hastings Ismay, expressing his enthusiasm for the use of raiding forces: 'how wonderful it would be if the Germans could be made to wonder where they were going to be struck next, instead of forcing us to try to wall in the island and roof over it'. Churchill's memoranda on this subject were welcomed by Lt Col Dudley Clarke, Military Assistant to the Chief of the Imperial General Staff (CIGS), Gen Sir John Dill. Clarke advocated 'hit and run' tactics normally associated with guerrilla warfare, and the use of irregular forces, which became known as commandos. This idea quickly gained traction for two reasons: first, given a Nazi-dominated Europe, and the threat of a German invasion of Britain, a full-scale invasion of the Continent could only be considered in the long term, hence the emphasis on raids; second, the notion of striking back at the enemy would boost morale on the home front.

Initially, the troops chosen for raiding were independent companies, some of which had taken part in the Norwegian campaign. The independent companies were later renamed commandos and formed into Special Service Battalions. On 14 June 1940, Lt Gen A.G.B. Bourne was given operational command of the independent companies and became adviser to the Chiefs-of-Staff on Combined Operations.

The phrase 'combined operations' as used by the Allies during World War II referred to operations that involved air, land or naval forces acting together. There was a famous precedent – the successful amphibious raid on Zeebrugge in 1918. The chief organizer of this raid, AF Sir Roger Keyes, was appointed as Director of Combined Operations on 17 July 1940 in succession to Gen Bourne. However, his overbearing personality caused tensions with the chiefs-of-staff and by October 1941 he had left, to be replaced by a cousin of the King, Capt Lord Louis Mountbatten, who was assigned the title of Adviser on Combined Operations on 27 October and promoted to commodore 1st class.

Raiding strategy

This appointment heralded a period of rapid reorganization, growth and activity at Combined Operations Headquarters (which up to this point had been on a small scale). A directive of 9 December 1941 tasked Mountbatten with studying 'tactical and technical developments in all forms of combined operations varying from small raids to a full-scale invasion of the Continent'. A strategy was devised, and this was developed further by Mountbatten, who argued that larger raids should be interspersed with minor ones, the latter being 'capable of being planned and mounted very quickly'. Mountbatten elaborated on his thinking: 'if repeated minor raids force him [the enemy] to keep his troops permanently in the "stand to" state, they will hereby achieve a definite object and may even detract from his state of alertness to meet the larger raids'.

Small-scale raids on the Boulogne area on 24–25 June 1940 (Operation *Collar*), and on Guernsey on 14–15 July 1940 (Operation *Ambassador*) achieved little and were, to some extent, shambolic, though lessons were learned about the need to be fully trained and supplied with suitable equipment and craft.

Churchill, however, was not satisfied with pinprick attacks to merely annoy the Germans – he wanted raids with much greater impact.

OPERATION *CLAYMORE*
Industrial sabotage in Norway's Lofoten Islands

The first successful Combined Operations raid was on the Lofoten Islands in Norway, also known as Operation *Claymore*, which took place on 4 March 1941.

The thinking behind the attack

On 17 January 1941, Hugh Dalton, Minister of Economic Warfare, wrote to Churchill proposing a surprise raid on the Lofoten Islands in northern Norway, which were the location of several herring and cod liver oil factories. These might seem a strange choice of target, but fish oil products were of great importance to the enemy, particularly capsules supplying vitamins A and D, which were deficient in the German diet at that time. What's more, fish oil also supplied the raw material for glycerine, used in the production of high explosives. Dalton therefore called for the oil plants to be destroyed, pointing out that 'the almost perpetual darkness will minimize the danger of air attack'.

Everything goes to plan

The proposal having been approved, the raid duly took place on 4 March 1941. The troops landed at four fishing ports on the south-east shores of the Lofoten Islands: No. 3 Commando went ashore at Stamsund and Henningsvaer, and No. 4 at Svolvaer and Brettesnes. No opposition was encountered, and the inhabitants gave the troops a warm welcome, despite the fact that the demolitions being carried out would seriously damage the livelihoods of the locals, which were mostly derived from their fishing industry.

Assisted by the Royal Engineers, the parties went on to destroy not only 16 factories but also several oil tanks in each port, along with their contents, amounting to 800,000 gallons. They also captured 12 Norwegian collaborators ('quislings'), and 213 enemy prisoners. More than 300 Norwegian volunteers

Map showing the planned
landings on the Lofoten
Islands. ▶

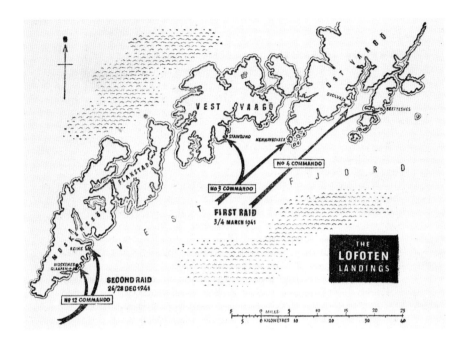

were brought back to Britain. The British forces themselves suffered no casualties – and had sunk shipping totalling 18,000 tons. Lt Col R.G. Parks-Smith of the Royal Marines described the scene as he sailed away: 'I remember most vividly the contrast between the brilliance of the snow and the black smoke and also the great height to which it rose.'

Fish oil tanks on the Lofoten
Islands, prior to Operation
Claymore. ▶

◀ A series of fish oil tanks ablaze following the attack.

The operation had been a complete success. Churchill was delighted – on 7 March he sent a message to the Commander-in-Chief Home Fleet, John Tovey: 'I am so glad you were able to find the means of executing *Claymore*. This admirable raid has done serious injury to the enemy and has given an immense amount of innocent pleasure at home.'

◀ Commandos stand watching the oil tanks burn.

OPERATION *ARCHERY*
Raiding industrial targets and German bases in Norway

Towards the end of September 1941, the chiefs-of-staff decided that operations against the German positions on the Norwegian coast should be carried out as soon as possible. Mountbatten's first assignment was therefore to draw up a Combined Operations plan to raid the Norwegian coast again, using the RAF to attack enemy airfields and give cover to surface forces.

A two-part scheme

The final plan had two components: for the main operation, *Archery*, the locations would be the islands of Vaagso and Maaloy; a diversionary raid, Operation *Anklet*, involved a return to the Lofoten Islands. The objectives were similar to those of Operation *Claymore*: to destroy German installations and shipping, and to disrupt fish-oil production. Notably, No. 3 Commando would deliberately set out to engage with the German garrison in the town of South Vaagso, an important harbour, and would aim to take complete control of the town.

The commandos trained very thoroughly prior to Operation *Archery* – though it should be pointed out that, with the exception of some officers, the men did not know anything about the location and details of the raid until the force started to assemble.

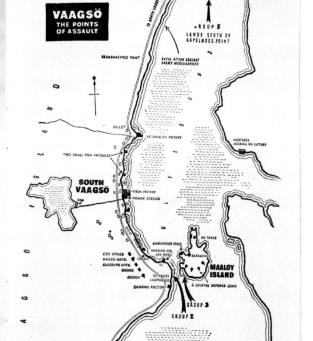

Plan of the proposed operation on the island of Vaagso. ▼

15

Setting the stage

The naval force, which set sail on Christmas Eve 1941, consisted of troop transport ships (the *Prince Charles* and *Prince Leopold*), supported by a naval escort of four destroyers, the cruiser HMS *Kenya* and a submarine. The force reached the Shetlands that day, but heavy weather and the need to pump out water from the *Prince Charles* and to make repairs to some of the infantry landing ships led to the operation being delayed for a day – enabling the men to enjoy their Christmas dinner. On the evening of Boxing Day,

Lord Mountbatten inspects the commandos before the commencement of Operation *Archery*. ▼

however, everything was ready: the force moved up Vaggs Fjord and the ships took up their positions.

Massive bombardment

By 08:35 on 27 December, the commandos had been loaded into their assault landing craft, ready to go ashore. At 08:48, HMS *Kenya* fired a salvo of 'star shells', which illuminated the island of Maaloy. This not only showed the target to the naval gunners, but it also indicated to the RAF Hampden

Commandos priming grenades during Operation Archery. ▼

bombers flying overhead the place where smoke bombs were to be dropped in order to provide cover for the landing forces – an objective they achieved at Rugsundo to the east. HMS *Kenya* and the other warships then delivered a massive bombardment directed at the German defences on Maaloy, which was also very precise; *Kenya* scored a direct hit on the gun battery. In retaliation, the battery at Maaloy opened fire on *Kenya*.

From post-operation reports based on interrogation of prisoners, it is clear that the Germans on Maaloy had been caught by surprise. The commanding officer's batman was on telephone duty (the phone was connected to the lookout post), but he was so busy cleaning his master's boots that when the telephone bell started to ring, he ignored it and did not answer. This was a key mistake since the person at the other end of the line had wanted to tell him that 'enemy ships were approaching'. Having not received the message, the German gunners did not know that bombardment was imminent.

▲ Reinforcement troops bein ferried over from Maaloy to help with the fighting in Sout Vaagso.

Fierce fighting

The landing craft made their way to their objectives. The force had been divided into five groups. Group 1 was to land near the village of Hollevik, on the southern shore of the island of Vaagso, clear the area and then move northwards to remain as reserve for Group 2. The largest group, consisting of some 200 men, was Group 2 and this would attack the town of South Vaagso. Group 3 was to capture Maaloy Island. Group 4 would remain in the landing craft as a floating reserve. Group 5 was to be taken by destroyer up Ulvesand and then landed between the towns of South and North Vaagso to cut communications between them.

Fires and explosions on Vaagso and Maaloy. ▼

Group 1 soon fulfilled its task. Group 2, meanwhile, landed very close to South Vaagso and advanced into the town, where they met fierce opposition. The Germans were now fully alert and defended themselves with great determination. Unfortunately for the commandos, the German garrison had been bolstered by some extra troops on their Christmas leave. House-to-house fighting ensued, with the added peril of highly effective and tenacious German snipers, with the result that there were several casualties among the commandos. A detachment of Group 2 went further north of the town and destroyed a herring oil factory.

Group 3 were rather more fortunate. Capt P. Young recalled: 'when we got near the island of Maaloy, Maj Churchill played the "March of the Cameron Men" on his bagpipes – cheered up the men wonderfully'. The group made rapid progress and found that three of the four coastal batteries had been destroyed by the bombardment. They commandeered the remaining one and turned its fire on a German flak ship, and went on to capture the whole island of Maaloy in less than half an hour. This accomplished, soon after

British troops examining a captured German gun on Maaloy. ▼

A burning oil factory on Vaagso, 1941. ▷

10:30, part of Group 3 re-entered their landing craft to go to the aid of their comrades in Group 2 in South Vaagso.

Those comrades were still hotly engaged in the bitter street fighting and were making slow progress, but the arrival of reinforcements from Groups 3 and 1 tipped the balance in favour of the commandos, who succeeded in crushing almost all opposition in South Vaagso by 12:30.

Commandos move through a smoke screen. ▷

◀ The shattered remains of a German barracks with an ammunition dump on fire.

A complete success

Virtually all the military and economic targets had been destroyed, including factories, munition dumps, oil tanks, military storehouses and a wireless station. The Germans suffered 150 killed as well as 98 captured. In a report, the morale of these prisoners of war was described as being very low: 'prisoners seemed utterly dejected or stunned as they were being ferried across to the ships' and conversations with four POWs were summed up as follows: 'they hated being in Vaagso – among people generally hostile to Germany, or isolated in the islet'.

In addition to the other successes, 77 loyal Norwegians accepted a passage to England; nine ships representing 15,000 tons of shipping were destroyed; and Blenheim bombers made a successful attack on Herdla, the nearest aerodrome, which put it out of service for enemy aircraft. The combined forces withdrew in the mid-afternoon of 27 December. An Admiralty communiqué stated: 'the operation was completely successful in all respects'.

The remains of a Norwegian oil factory following the assault.

OPERATION *ANKLET*
Disrupting German communications in Norway

While the raid on South Vaagso was taking place, a diversionary raid was being carried out on the Lofoten Islands (Operation *Anklet*). Although this raid could be described as relatively minor, the plan was actually ambitious, though rather vaguely formulated (particularly regarding its likely duration).

Everything goes to plan

The intention was to use Skjelfjord as a temporary anchorage and Kirkefjord as a fuelling base for Combined Ops forces operating against the enemy's lines of communication within northern Norway, 'as long as conditions render this possible'. The main military force consisted of No. 12 Commando, along with some Norwegian personnel, under CO Lt Col S.S. Harrison, MC. Their main object was to temporarily occupy the towns of Reine and Moskenes.

Force J (the main force) sailed from Scapa Flow on 22 December. In the course of carrying out a sweep up the fjord, the principal naval force captured two Norwegian coastal steamers and sank an armed German trawler. Four landing operations were carried out on 26 December and the Belgian infantry assault ship, *Prince Albert*, reached Reine at the mouth of Kirkefjord. Here, the landing force of more than 100 men included Special Operations Executive (SOE) personnel under Maj Torrance, who, for a short time, made Reine a centre for distributing comforts to Norwegians, and arresting Germans and collaborators. A successful raid was also made on the wireless stations at Glaapen and Savargen, and several German prisoners were taken.

During the course of these activities, raiding forces found plenty of Christmas treats at Glaapen (large rations of chocolate, cigarettes and coffee), which they promptly distributed to the local inhabitants, who, according to an account on file, 'cheered continually and shook hands with the troops, asking them to stay or take them home with us'.

Premature withdrawal

It was not all chocolate and good cheer, however, since the naval force had been spotted by an enemy reconnaissance plane. In consequence, on 27 December, a German seaplane dropped a bomb very close to the headquarters ship HMA *Arethusa*; it seemed that the high mountains did not offer the protection against air attack that had been hoped for. After receiving reports that the Germans were amassing more aircraft for an attack, R Adm Hamilton therefore decided on a withdrawal on 28 December.

Despite its curtailed duration, 29 German prisoners and six quislings were taken, and 266 Norwegian refugees were evacuated. In retaliation, the Germans arrested all Norwegian officers.

Self-censorship

Capt Pinckney and Capt Jefferies explain why they threw the films overboard following Operation *Anklet*. ▼

The story of the operation doesn't end there, as an unusual episode occurred on the return journey. The incident involved Capts Jeffreys and Pinckney of

```
                                             No. 12 Commando
                                             H.M.S. PRINCE ALBERT
  To:  Officer Commanding,                   31.Dec. '41
       No. 12 Commando

  From Capt. J. B. Jefferies
       Capt. P. Pinckney

            Our reasons for destroying the pictorial records of the
       expedition are as follows:-

            On learning of our presence in the Lofoten Islands the
       inhabitants were at first considerably perturbed owing to the
       retribution which the Germans had made on Svolvaer and Stamsund
       after the last raid.  When however they were given to understand
       that we should remain until the scale of the German attack became
       too great, they co-operated to their fullest extent.  Films taken
       of our occupation of their friendliness and willingness to help.

            On our premature departure, they all felt they had been
       betrayed and they wept and cursed us to a man.  This treacherous
       side of such an ignominious expedition was not filmed.

            We felt that there was every danger of films and
       photographs being made public, which apart from its complete
       deception of the British people, would seriously add to the
       incredible damage already done to Anglo-Norwegian relations
       by what one Norwegian so rightly described as a "very cheap
       demonstration."

                                        ((Sd.) J. B. JEFFERIES , Capt.

                                         "  P. H. PINCKNEY, Capt.
```

No. 12 Commando, who threw films belonging to the official press contingent into the sea, prompting a strong complaint from Lt L.A. Puttnam, Official War Photographer. In defence, Capts Jefferies and Pinckney justified their actions in a report submitted to CO Harrison who, when he interviewed Lt Col Harrison, appeared to show some sympathy with his men's actions, while simultaneously stating in a message that 'the incident is regretted'.

One possible cause of both the captains' actions and the CO's sympathy with them was that Churchill was very unhappy at the outcome of the operation, which he called 'a marked failure', so perhaps the men wanted to dispose of any reminders of the mission. Churchill had expected a much more rigorous plan in terms of anti-aircraft provision and a much longer stay on the Lofoten Islands, neither of which came to pass.

OPERATION *BITING*
Attacking German radar installations in France: Bruneval, 1942

The invention of radar enabled the RAF to detect aircraft by sending out pulses of radio waves that were reflected off object(s) back to the source. This system made a significant contribution to the RAF's success in the Battle of Britain in 1940, enabling the RAF to track incoming German planes, and was part of an early warning system. British intelligence had been aware that Germany also possessed some form of radar in 1940, but there was a lack of detailed information available about this development. Over time, intelligence sources identified that a system called Freya was utilized in France, and that this was, in some cases, being combined with a new type of radar operating on a short range, Würzburg, which refined the tracking of aircraft.

By late 1941, Germany had also made considerable progress in the field of radio waves and had established a radar network along the coastline of western Europe. This allowed them to successfully detect British aircraft as they approached the French coast and was a major factor behind heavy Bomber Command losses. There was the potential for British scientists to develop counter-measures, but in order to do this, they needed to analyse the components of the Würzburg apparatus. The only solution was to steal the key parts of such a structure and bring them back to England for examination.

Superb aerial reconnaissance

RAF Photographic Reconnaissance were tasked with finding a Würzburg installation and on 15 November 1941 took a photograph that excited the interest of scientists Dr R.V. Jones and his assistant, Dr F.C. Frank. The photograph revealed that there was a Freya station on top of the cliffs at La Poterie-Cap-d'Antifer, near Bruneval, some 10 miles north of Le Havre. The scientists noticed a small black object in front of a large villa, and they wondered if it could be radar apparatus. So, on 5 December 1941, Flt Lt Tony Hill carried out photographic reconnaissance over the site – a risky operation – and succeeded in capturing a very detailed image that confirmed suspicions. A plan thus began to be formulated for a raid, with the aim of stealing the radar equipment.

The photograph which first excited the interest of the scientists. ▼

OM
PLACEMENTS

SMALL BLACK OBJECT

In January 1942, Lord Louis Mountbatten, Chief of Combined Operations, proposed using airborne forces, and once this had been agreed, it was decided to use the newly formed 1st Airborne Division, the final choice for the mission being C Company of the recently formed 2nd Parachute Battalion, commanded by Maj John Frost. Eight Royal Engineers would also take part, including Flt Sgt Cox, a radar specialist, who underwent an intensive and highly compressed programme of parachute training.

The plan for this mission had several elements and was a truly 'combined' operation, involving the RAF and Royal Navy. The paratroopers, 120 in total, would be flown to Bruneval by 12 Whitley bombers and dropped inland, some distance from the isolated villa. The paratroopers would then be split into various parties, with specific tasks, the most important of which was to dismantle and take away the key components of the Würzburg apparatus. Once this key objective had been achieved, the men would pull back to the small beach nearby to be taken off by landing craft from the support ship *Prinz Albert*. In addition, the RAF was tasked with providing fighter cover for the operation.

erial photograph of the
ürzburg target prior to the
uneval raid. ▶

Pre-war photo of the beach at Bruneval.

The rubber model made of the Bruneval raid site as part of planning for the operation. ▼

Thorough preparations

The preparations for the raid were amazingly thorough. On 4 January 1942, Combined Operations contacted the Air Ministry to ask for a model of the site to be raided, stipulating that it had to be approximately 5 sq ft, and show 'full details of houses, woods, paths, fissures in cliffs'. The Air Intelligence Department duly produced a model to these requirements that was truly remarkable in its attention to detail. In a personal account of the raid, Maj Frost, referring to landing on the site and finding the meeting-up place, commented: 'the reason why we arrived just where we wanted to go was in great part due to the excellent air photography... and to the model of the country which every man had studied, so that we all knew what to expect'.

Brave spirit

Personal accounts of the raid, which took place on 27–28 February 1942, help us to understand what it was like to take part in such an operation and give insights into the brave spirit of the troops involved. Here is Maj Frost again, commenting on the morale of the paratroopers on the way to Bruneval: 'in our aircraft we were cheerful; we sang songs and played cards, chiefly pontoon. Spirits were very high; indeed, I can describe them as terrific.' According to Flt Sgt Charles Cox: 'we sang among other things the parachute song, which begins "Come sit by my side if you love me"'. He continues: 'as I am reputed to have something of a voice I sang a solo, "The Rose of Tralee"'. This was a man who had undergone parachute training only very recently, who was about to be dropped into enemy-occupied (and snow-covered) territory at night, on a vital mission, with a great deal of responsibility resting on his shoulders, singing an Irish ballad to entertain his comrades (and, no doubt, to help counter any nerves).

The operation, which was carried out in bright moonlight, generally went according to plan, except that one aircraft dropped its parachutists out of position. Mountbatten later reported: 'this proved a fortunate mistake as they came in in the flank of the German opposition and helped to clear up the situation'. Maj Frost's assault party attacked the isolated house, and found only one German there, who was killed. Meanwhile, a party led by Lt Young was in the process of capturing the radio location station. Young and his men killed five Germans found in the dugouts there (their orders were that only experts should be taken prisoner, and the remainder were to be killed). One German, who turned out to be a radar operator, tried to hide near the cliff edge and then, according to a report filed by Wg Cdr Felkin, 'accidentally slipped over and fell about 15 feet before he could save himself by grasping

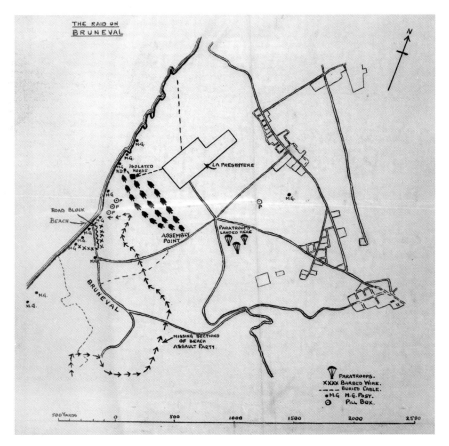

◀ Sketch map of the Brunev
raid.

a projecting rock'. The radar operator was then helped back over by a paratroop officer and taken prisoner.

Under fire

By this time, the Germans, including personnel housed at nearby Le Presbytere, were fully alert to the raid and the British troops were under machine-gun fire. Elsewhere, a party of sappers led by Lt Vernon had moved up to the Würzburg, which was secure, and Sgt Cox and the remainder of the sappers had been notified to come forwards to do their work. Sgt Cox and sapper Cpl Jones duly went about dismantling the Würzburg – something that was no easy feat; they had to use force after their tools had failed – with bullets flying too close for comfort. Eventually, they somehow succeeded in nearly all respects and were able to carry away key parts of the apparatus using trolleys they had brought for that purpose, although these proved difficult to manoeuvre in the snow and were eventually abandoned.

Maj Frost, meanwhile, ordered his men to withdraw towards the beach – a retreat that involved more fierce fighting since the beach had not yet been secured. The reason for this was that the party of men tasked with

British troops search German prisoners captured after Operation *Biting*. ▼

capturing it had been dropped about 2½ miles from the assembly point, had enemy forces to deal with, and were therefore late in arriving. However, despite these unforeseen difficulties, the parties did manage to link up, a German strongpoint was eliminated and the men were able to get down to the beach to await the Navy.

Once on the beach, the threat scarcely diminished and there were some anxious moments when signs were spotted that enemy reinforcements were on their way. Despite these, Maj Frost agreed that a signal be sent to the Navy that it was safe to come into shore, so Very lights (flares) were sent up into the sky, and the landing craft were sent in. It was 02:35 and it had been a truly 'lightning' raid, lasting only two hours. The flotilla made for England, and once day had dawned it was given air cover by RAF Spitfires, and arrived safely back in home waters.

In all, two raiders were killed in the operation and six were reported missing. Two German prisoners were brought back, one of which was the radar operator. According to a report entitled 'The Intelligence Aspect of the Bruneval Raid', 'the prisoner [the radar operator] was rather childlike and extremely unsoldierly in mentality'. Another report states: 'P/W is very willing to impart all he knows, but is of limited intelligence'. Nonetheless, he did provide some useful information about the way the radar system operated, and his poor skill level reflected the lack of priority given to the radar-monitoring task by Nazi Germany.

A great success

Operation *Biting* was judged by the military authorities to have been a great success. British scientists were impressed by the quality of German RDF construction but were also reassured to find nothing truly innovative in the captured apparatus. They analysed the equipment very carefully, probing it for weak points, to see if it could be vulnerable to counter-measures, such as jamming. The knowledge gained through the Bruneval raid, combined with further reconnaissance, prompted the use of 'window' – the dropping of small aluminium strips that had the effect of clouding German radar, a tactic first used by the RAF in July 1943 during a major raid on Hamburg.

OPERATION *CHARIOT*
Stopping the mighty *Tirpitz*: the raid on St-Nazaire

Commissioned in 1941, the *Tirpitz* was the largest battleship of Nazi Germany's Kriegsmarine (Navy) during World War II. In January 1942, the battleship was sent to Trondheim, Norway so that it could be used to attack the Russia-bound Arctic convoys. The British were particularly concerned about the potential danger this move posed as it signified a very real threat to Britain's supply lines, so they started to think of ways to prevent the battleship from being used against British shipping.

If the *Tirpitz* were damaged, the only port able to accommodate her for repair work would be St-Nazaire, which contained the vast Normandie Dock (*La Forme-écluse Joubert*) – the largest dry dock in the world when it opened in 1932, having been built to house the ocean liner *Normandie*. If the dock could somehow be put out of action, the thinking went, this would significantly reduce the risk of the *Tirpitz* being deployed in the Atlantic.

The Normandie Dock built to house the great liner SS *Normandie*, seen here in the dock. ▼

Naval Planning and Intelligence therefore started to consider an operation against St-Nazaire as early as July 1941, though only limited progress was made. In January 1942, however, the Chief of Combined Operations, Lord Louis Mountbatten, was asked to revive the plans.

It was not an easy prospect; St-Nazaire is situated some 6 miles up the Loire estuary and could only be approached from the sea by a narrow channel that was covered by several gun batteries. However, a study revealed a flaw in the port defences: during the high-water spring tides, a ship of shallow draught would be able to pass over the mud flats in the Loire estuary, rather than having to approach the docks through the shipping channel, which was heavily protected. The plan for the raid went through several modifications but was eventually finalized around mid-March 1942.

An ambitious plan

This was a raid with highly ambitious objectives: first, the destruction of the two caissons (huge watertight chambers) of the Normandie Dock; second, the demolition of dockyard facilities supporting the dry dock; third, the wrecking of all lock gates; and fourth, to attack any shipping – particularly U-boats, which were often stationed at St-Nazaire – in special pens.

The plan was that the expendable destroyer, HMS *Campbeltown*, would sail up the Loire estuary as part of a flotilla, having first been stripped of all non-essential items to make it sufficiently light to take advantage of the tides, though there was one extra item on board: tons of explosives in the forward compartments. The ship's mission was to ram the lock gates, whereupon the ship would be scuttled and a delayed-action fuse would be used to explode the huge charge. Demolition parties of commandos would then land from the ship, with specific tasks to put dockyard facilities and mechanisms out of action. The other military forces, meanwhile, would arrive in motor launches, which would also be used for the withdrawal.

Surprise – and disguise – were seen as crucial elements, and to this end *Campbeltown* was altered to resemble a German destroyer, with modifications to her funnels. In the skies above, the RAF was ordered to launch a diversionary bombing attack at the same time as the raid, to draw the attention of the German gunners. This was deemed a critical factor – indeed, Mountbatten said that the success of the operation depended on it.

As ambitious as it was audacious, this was a truly high-risk operation. The motor launches, motor gun and motor torpedo boats were highly vulnerable thanks to two factors: first, the ships had thin wooden sides, which offered no protection against bullets and salvoes; and second, tanks of petrol had been mounted on their decks in order to enable the craft to make it to St-Nazaire and back, and these could easily explode.

Cdr Robert Ryder, RN, was appointed to command the naval craft and, as most of the military forces were drawn from No. 2 Commando, the officer commanding that unit, Lt Col Charles Newman, became the Military Commander. The *Campbeltown* was to be under the command of Lt Cdr Stephen Beattie.

Maintaining the element of surprise

The flotilla embarked from Falmouth on the afternoon of 26 March, steering clear of the French coast on that day in order to mislead the enemy as to its purpose. The remainder of the day was uneventful, but early on the morning of 27 March the destroyer HMS *Tynedale* spotted a U-boat (*U-593*), which was pursued and depth-charged. The U-boat disappeared and her destruction was not confirmed. Obviously it would be catastrophic if the element of surprise, so vital to the operation's success, had been lost, but despite the uncertainty, Cdr Ryder considered that the voyage should continue.

In fact, *U-593* had survived the encounter, but its commander gave an inaccurate report to German command, reporting that the flotilla was heading west, when it was actually starting to head south-east at the time of the incident. German command therefore thought that the flotilla might be en route to Gibraltar, or could be engaged in laying mines, so fortunately for the British their plan was not foiled by this encounter.

Soon after this episode, however, the British flotilla encountered a flotilla of French fishing trawlers, which had to be dealt with; once the fishermen had been taken on board the destroyers, the vessels were sunk – no risks could be taken regarding any possibility of security being compromised.

The flotilla enters the Loire

At 22:00, a red light was spotted ahead of the flotilla. This belonged to the British submarine *Sturgeon*, acting as a navigation beacon to guide the force in. The flotilla slid past, took up the attack formation and entered the Loire.

At about midnight, the RAF raid on St-Nazaire began. The force consisted of 35 Whitleys and 26 Wellingtons. They encountered bad weather over the target area – severe cloud cover and icing within the cloud – which meant that only three aircraft felt sufficiently sure, owing to temporary breaks in the cloud, that they were in the target area and could drop their bombs. Nevertheless, the planes circled overhead, hoping to distract the German gunners as the flotilla continued its progress. Despite their presence, though, the tension aboard the naval vessels must have been palpable, as it was surely only a matter of time before the raiding force was discovered.

All seemed well, however, and the flotilla continued and made remarkably good progress, safely passing German checkpoints. Then, at 01:20, with the force less than 2 miles from the target, the German garrison commander sent out an alert to the coastal batteries and every available searchlight focused on the dark waters of the estuary, soon picking out the *Campbeltown* and her fleet of small ships. This was when the disguise element of the plan came into its own. Seeing that the *Campbeltown* resembled a German destroyer and was bearing a German flag, the Germans hesitated. A warning shot was fired over the flotilla, and German signallers demanded recognition. The motor gun boat (MGB), which was leading the line, responded by signalling (using German call signs) that two ships had been damaged by enemy action, and asked for permission to proceed to harbour without delay. This action, which seemed to placate the German defenders, gained the flotilla valuable minutes before the Germans started to fire again. The MGB responded by making the enemy signal for a vessel under 'friendly fire', a tactic that also gained the force respite, for a few moments at least.

Full fury of the guns

The game of bluff couldn't last forever, however, and it came to an abrupt end as the Germans realized this was a hostile force. Now, every German gun battery opened fire – and every ship fired back. The crew of the *Campbeltown* lowered the German flag and raised the White Ensign – a stirring moment. In his personal account of the raid, Cdr Ryder wrote: 'it is difficult to describe the full fury of the attack that was let loose on each side … the night became one mass of red and green tracer'.

The enemy guns hit the *Campbeltown* repeatedly on just about every level and casualties mounted. Regardless, Cdr Beattie made for the dock gates

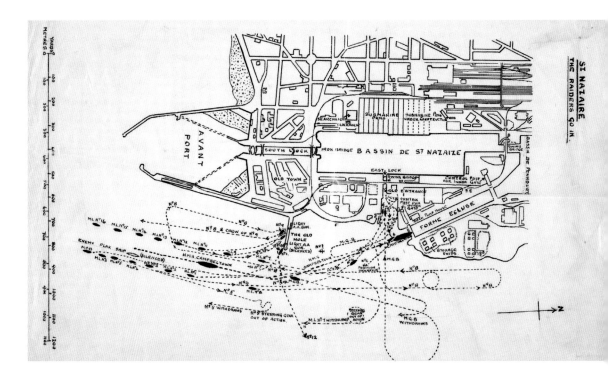

with all speed, and the old destroyer cut through the anti-submarine net and rammed into the dock gates, coming to rest there with the bows of the ship rearing over the gates; the explosives in her forward sections were thus well placed. Lt Col Newman later described Beattie's seamanship as 'a superlative

▲ Map showing the route of the raiders at St-Nazaire.

◀ Artist's impression of HMS *Campbeltown* running into the dock gates at St-Nazaire.

feat', praise that is attested to by the fact that *Campbeltown* struck the dock gates at 01:34 – just four minutes later than scheduled.

At this stage, commandos on board the *Campbeltown* scrambled down ladders to get ashore and to set about their demolition tasks, eliminating machine-gun placements in the process. They went on to successfully attack their chief objectives: dockyard equipment, mechanisms and fuel stores.

Dreadful conditions

On the estuary, meanwhile, conditions for the motor launches were hellish. Enemy guns had set fire to or sunk many of them. Lt Col Newman later wrote:

> The fact that the MLs had to carry such a large deck cargo of petrol caused the majority of their sinkings. These petrol containers were hit and the ships blew up.

Some of the British troops captured at St-Nazaire. ▼

The whole river was a mass of burning petrol on the water and many men lost their lives either burnt to death or drowned in it. Without this potential danger, I believe that in spite of the heavy fire, the MLs could have got in to take us off.

The launches were intended as the commandos' means of escape, but with so many destroyed, Newman now gave orders to the men to make a break for it, the plan being to head for open country and to try to escape via Spain to England (five men succeeded in doing this). He also ordered his men not to surrender until all ammunition had been used.

In all, just four motor launches escaped the estuary, although one was subsequently caught by a German torpedo boat. The others successfully linked up with the destroyers. In addition to the loss of motor launches, human casualties were high – of the 611 who took part in the mission, 169 were killed and 214 were taken prisoner. However, the operation was successful. The time fuses attached to the explosives on board did their work, albeit with a longer delay than expected, and at 10:35 on 28 March the *Campbeltown* suddenly exploded, killing a group of German officers on board at the time, and putting the dry dock out of action for the rest of the war.

As a result, the St-Nazaire raid became known as 'the greatest raid of all' for its sheer audacity, a point reinforced by the contemporary German reaction, as reported by Lt Stuart Chant of No. 5 Commando, who described this exchange following his capture: 'I was asked by a German officer through an interpreter who was a German sailor, "How the hell did you ever manage to get up here." I replied "We just got here" and the German said "Well it beats us how you managed it". The surprise of the Germans was most marked.'

Postscript

Because of the delay before the *Campbeltown* exploded, on the morning of 28 March the Nazis were convinced that the raid had been a failure. The Nazi propaganda machine was, of course, keen to exploit this angle. National Archives files include transcripts of German radio broadcasts, and a fascinating story emerges from one particular example. It begins: 'It has been a hectic night: the British have attempted a raid on the French Coast at St-Nazaire. But the attempt was a failure … now we are here down below in the harbour and should expect a patrol boat … bringing back some prisoners of war taken off a sunken torpedo boat'. The vessel arrives, carrying survivors, many of whom are injured. The commentator says, with synthetic sympathy, 'they have been through a tremendous strain … the police will be taking them to the G'PO [Gestapo] where they will furnish them with new clothes and will take care of their injuries'. The Gestapo portrayed as caring and humanitarian!

There then follows a series of interviews with the British soldiers. The men sound amazingly cheery, e.g. 'Hullo [*sic*], Mrs Jones of 72 Enfield Road, Blakely, Manchester. It's Arthur speaking. I'm quite well and happy.' There is also a conversation with an officer who seems surprisingly cooperative in talking about the raid, going well beyond giving name, rank and number. This prompts the question: why are the men being so open?

The answer is provided by Lt Stuart Chant, who was recorded in the exchanges and, once repatriated, gave an explanation of what had happened:

> After our capture those of us who were wounded were taken to a German Naval Hospital … after a few days a party arrived in plain clothes … stating they were Red X [Cross] officials … we were invited to give our names and addresses of our next of kin, with any short messages that we might like forwarded … it was not until some time later when we had official visits from real Red X officials that we realized that the original party … must have been completely bogus … I can only assume that our voices were picked up by microphones hidden in the hospital and recorded for broadcast later.

However, this explanation still leaves questions unanswered, as when one reads the transcript, it seems that the men knew they were being recorded. An element of mystery therefore still surrounds this episode. Whatever the truth, though, the broadcast – however it was compiled – certainly reflects ingenuity on the part of Goebbels' propaganda machine.

OPERATION *JUBILEE*
Attacking German defences in France: the Dieppe Raid

From the time of Mountbatten's appointment as Adviser on Combined Operations in late October 1941, a great momentum had been achieved, with the successful raids on Vaagso, Bruneval and St-Nazaire boosting the confidence of Combined Operations. Demands therefore began to mount for an assault on enemy-occupied territory on a far larger scale.

In the first half of 1942 the situation facing the Allies was bleak: Singapore had fallen to the Japanese on 15 February; the British garrison at Tobruk in North Africa surrendered on 21 June; German U-boats were taking a terrible toll on Allied vessels in the Atlantic, and the Russians were hard pressed along the entire Eastern Front.

The idea of a raid on Dieppe, on the coast of northern France, was conceived in early April 1942 at Combined Operations Headquarters against a background of mounting military and political pressures. The official justification was to prepare for the invasion of France – to gain valuable experience of amphibious assault under modern conditions, and to test the strength of German defences. Churchill was later to refer to the Dieppe Raid as a 'reconnaissance in force'. However, there was also a political motive: Stalin was demanding the opening up of a second front in Western Europe as soon as possible, so that German forces in the east would be moved west.

The majority of the land force for this operation was to be supplied by Canadian troops. The Canadian 2nd Division had been stationed in Britain since December 1940 and by mid-1942 many Canadian soldiers were bored with the constant routine of training and were restless for action.

A complicated scheme
Following a study of the options, the chiefs-of-staff approved the outline plan on 13 May. It was highly complicated. First, the coastal batteries (a threat to

the main amphibious force) were to be eliminated by No. 4 Commando (to the west) and No. 3 Commando (to the east). Both of these units were to attack at 04:50. At the same time, the flanking towns of Pourville (to the west) and Puys (to the east) were to be attacked by Canadian infantry regiments. At 05:20, the main force would then make a frontal attack on the port itself, landing infantry forces. Landing craft tank (LCT) would bring the new Churchill tanks ashore, whereupon tanks and infantry were to attack and ultimately take control of the town.

Originally, a major pre-assault air bombardment of the town had been planned, but this was scaled down to fighter attacks on German beach defences and the high ground to the east and west of Dieppe just prior to the landings, and diversionary bombing attacks on German airfields.

Nevertheless, there were still some 16 military objectives in total, stretching a considerable way inland; it truly was an audacious scheme. In fact, one of the chief criticisms of the Dieppe Raid was that it was overambitious in conception.

Intelligence and preparation

On the surface level, the use of photographic intelligence during the preparations for the Dieppe Raid seemed very thorough. The Combined Operations HQ records reveal that the large-scale aerial reconnaissance carried out in May 1942 'was a difficult and dangerous commitment to accept' and 'met with considerable enemy opposition'. Having been obtained despite these difficulties, the aerial photographs and maps resulting from the reconnaissance flights were prepared by the Central Interpretation Unit at Medmenham.

The aerial photograph collage of the Port of Dieppe and the related plan appear impressive regarding its high level of detail. A German report on the raid, captured by the Allies and translated in February 1944, commented that 'the British had at their disposal excellent maps on which all the information obtained from aerial reconnaissance was plotted'.

Another example that shows the level of preparation for the raid is the photograph of a model showing the coastal profile of Dieppe. Models such as this were used to produce silhouettes of the coast, photographed at very low angle from seaward, to represent the appearance of the coast at nautical twilight. These silhouettes, with the chosen landing places marked up, were issued to flotilla leaders and officers commanding all ships as an aid to recognition of the coastline.

C.B. 04157 F.

The photographs and maps that can be found among the planning documents certainly appear comprehensive in their scope. The tone of the captured German report is incredulous in this regard: 'it is astonishing that the British should have underestimated our defence, as they had the details of most of it from air photos'.

However, Allied intelligence did *not* have crucial details. In particular, the planners did not give adequate attention to the caves on either side of Dieppe harbour, which hid heavy machine guns and sniper positions. A series of concrete bunkers linked by trenches had been constructed on the beach at Dieppe; there were many pillboxes and roadblocks; and there was a significant

▲ The model showing the coastal profile of Dieppe and the area's defences.

Map showing the proposed area of battle. ▼

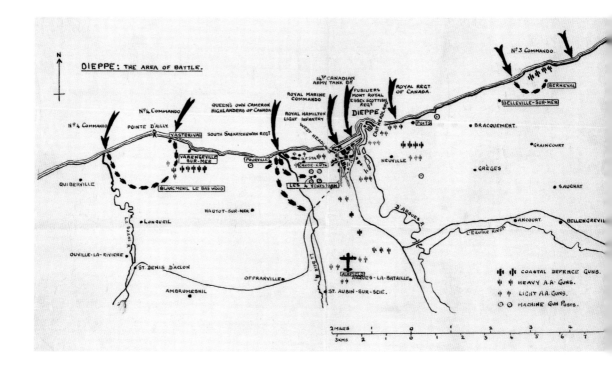

array of barbed wire. The photographs and maps therefore gave only a partial picture of the armaments and defences that were actually in place.

The raid, originally known as Operation *Rutter*, had been planned to take place at the end of June. Following postponements due to an unsuccessful exercise and poor weather, on 7 July it was abandoned and the troops dispersed. However, it was soon decided to remount the operation, with some modifications, under the code name *Jubilee*.

Operation *Jubilee* begins

The operation finally went ahead on the evening of 18 August, when some 250 ships sailed from Portsmouth, Southampton, Shoreham and Newhaven. Personal accounts of the journey of the flotilla are very effective in describing what it felt like to take part, such as this one by Acting Temp Sgt J.D. Cooke, RM:

> At last darkness came, and with it a brief respite. Gun stations were cleared, and the decks stripped for action. The ghostly figures of Commandos slid by on the jetty, moving with unnatural silence in their rubber-soled boots ... Hands fall into action stations – and the engines awoke to life. Moorings cast off, we slid away from the jetty into mid-stream, following the dim outlines of the ships preceding us. Soon we felt the easy motion of the Channel swell, and made our rendezvous with the rest of the flotilla at approximately 2230. So the small, tense, ghostly convoy slid on, the guns crews swaying with the motion of the ship, eyes alert for signs of action.

The journey was straightforward until landing craft containing No. 3 Commando encountered a German convoy off Dieppe. Several landing craft were sunk and damaged in the exchanges that followed – an incident that alerted the German defences at Puys.

A tragedy unfolds

The tale of the operation was almost unremittingly one of disaster. Only one action was completely successful: the assault on the cliff on the outer western front, in which No. 4 Commando, led by Lord Lovat, captured and destroyed a German coastal battery. On the outer eastern front, No. 3 Commando were pinned down by heavy fire on the beach and suffered heavy losses, and, unable to get off the beach, those who remained had little choice but to surrender.

The frontal assault met with resistance far stronger than had been expected and the troops were mown down by withering fire. Accounts in war diaries give a vivid picture of the horror and carnage that took place on the beaches, as shown by this extract from the diary for the 1st Royal Regiment of Canada, describing the scene as their landing craft came ashore at Puys ('Blue Beach'):

> As the first wave touched down and the doors opened, and the men rushed out, a hail of automatic fire opened from both flanks, and many men fell a few feet from where they disembarked. A few men were able to reach the beach wall which was about twelve feet high, and which afforded them some protection from the murderous cross-fire.

Referring to the 'Edward' force, which had landed to the east, the war diary entry continues: 'As no one returned from this force, details are vague, but it appears that the cliff was too steep to climb, and the force was discovered by the enemy, who dropped grenades from the heights with the result that casualties were probably heavy, and that no one, at any rate, was able to return'.

Many extraordinary stories of bravery can be found among the records of the Dieppe Raid, including this letter from Lt Col F.K. Jasperson, who commanded the Essex Scottish Regiment, written while in German captivity, addressed to his banker:

> I do want it known that the personal acts of bravery in this show are beyond words … Major Willis was undoubtedly outstanding. Badly wounded in chest, arms and head he carried on directing his company when it seemed humanly impossible to do so; and I'm sure when he received his last wound it was due to his effort in trying to bring a man back to safety. Lt Green with a foot shot off had it bound up and continued to hobble on leading his platoon until a second bomb finished him.

No significant progress was made by the infantry or the tanks (many of which became stranded on the beaches, unable to cope with the shingle). Instead, a withdrawal took place under terrible conditions and was completed by 14:00. The number of casualties was staggering: 3,367 killed, wounded or taken prisoner.

The Royal Air Force's role in the raid

The RAF saw the Dieppe Raid as an opportunity to engage with the Luftwaffe and wield significant damage. In a report on the RAF's involvement, AVM Leigh-Mallory referred to it as 'the greatest air fight the world has ever known'. There were four main areas of air support: first, fighter cover and general

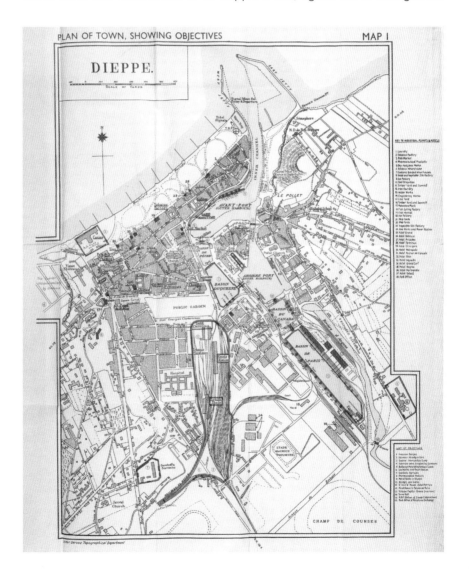

an of Dieppe, showing
e multiple objectives of
e raid. ▶

protection for the raiding forces throughout the areas of daylight (protection against air attack); second, close support and low-flying fighter attacks on selected targets, and smoke-laying aircraft were to be used to neutralize defences; third, reconnaissance over the area of the operation; and fourth, strategic bombing in the form of an air attack against the enemy aerodrome of Abbeville, to interfere with the enemy's defending fighters.

The National Archives holds a fascinating plan depicting the air operation from the Combined Report. This was drawn up after the operation, and shows the internal movements of RAF squadrons from stations in England. Each large aircraft represents a squadron and in the key the aircraft are coloured individually to indicate the type of aircraft (Spitfire, Hurricane, Fortress etc). The key also indicates the role of each type of aircraft (e.g. cover, close support, strategic bombing). The small aircraft each represent a single aircraft, so one can even trace the route of a single reconnaissance aircraft from Hawkinge in Kent right along the French coastline, past Dieppe, and on to Le Havre. Each aircraft represents one squadron sortie. The key states that the total number of aircraft sorties carried out on 18–19 August was 2,614, which underlines the sheer scale of the RAF operation.

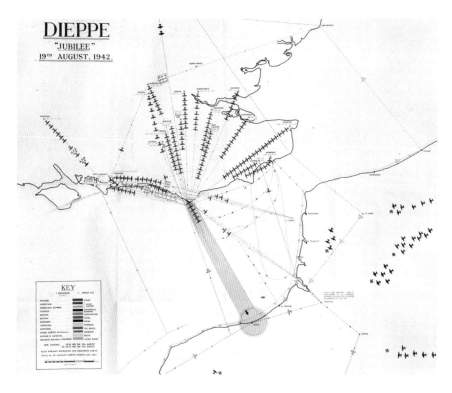

◀ Plan for the air operation on 19 August 1942.

Smoke from a fire burning on the front during the *Jubilee* operation. ▶

A Boston flies over France during Operation *Jubilee*. ▼

The initial bombing raids were ineffective and had little effect on German gun positions. Dogfights with enemy fighters started to develop, particularly from 08:30, and these continued throughout the day. Increasing numbers of German aircraft arrived as the morning went on, with the result that the air battle became intensive and raged for many hours.

◀ Troops on board a ship relaxing between orders.

Canadian troops being briefed prior to the operation.

A great air victory?

Initially, Combined Operations HQ and RAF Fighter Command claimed a great air victory. In a Chief of the Air Staff file there is a letter from Combined Operations Chief Louis Mountbatten to Air Chf Mshl Sir Charles Portal, dated 22 August 1942. It reads: 'I have now received sufficient preliminary reports to realize what a really wonderful show the Royal Air Force put up during the battle of Dieppe.' He sums up: 'Dieppe sets a new standard in air co-operation with the Army and the Navy which the Germans might have equalled but could hardly have surpassed.'

The same file contains a paragraph on enemy casualties that reads: 'the combat claims are not yet fully assessed, but the latest figures of 92 destroyed, 39 probably destroyed and 140 damaged are not expected to be materially altered'. However, the report warned about the need to treat figures with caution due to unavoidable duplication in claims.

A more sober assessment emerges from *The Air Defence of Great Britain, Volume 5: the Struggle for Air Supremacy* compiled by the Air Historical Branch after the war. Here it was admitted 'our claims were greatly over assessed' and 'our losses were … more than three times as heavy as the enemy's'. However, arguments for and against the air operation are set out in a finely balanced manner in this source. While accepting that 'the situation for the enemy was never really critical', the report concludes:

> From the point of view of Fighter Command, it might even be said Jubilee was a success … the Command had shown that it could provide effective day light cover for naval and military forces over seventy miles away from the English coast … in 1942 such a fact could not be taken for granted; nor could any invasion plans be prepared without such an assumption.

The Ian Fleming connection

It is a little-known fact that Ian Fleming, creator of James Bond and a Naval Intelligence officer, was present during the Dieppe Raid, though only as an observer. Fleming and others had originated the idea of 'Intelligence' commandos, based on German units, and this materialized into 30 Assault Unit – a team of commandos who were given a top-secret mission at Dieppe, under the unit name 40 Royal Marine Commando. Their task was to enter a hotel at Dieppe that was thought to be the German Naval Headquarters and to take away Enigma enciphering machines and associated documentation.

As Fleming tried to discern what was happening through the smoke, 40 Royal Marine Commando, on HMS *Locust*, were put into landing craft but failed to reach the main beach due to the massive barrage of German shells and bullets. No Enigma-related material was obtained.

Propaganda

German propaganda was quick to exploit the raid's failure. A four-page leaflet was dropped by German aircraft at night over the areas of Canadian camps

The German Propaganda leaflet that was dropped over southern England, showing photographs of the aftermath of the Dieppe Raid. ▶

Dieppe

We and British invade France.

(American Journal)

in southern England. It displays images of wrecked tanks and landing craft and the dead, wounded and captured. The quote on the front page, attributed to an American journal – 'We and British invade France' – is obviously heavily ironic in this context.

The photographs are carefully chosen, and carry the message that these are battle-weary but spirited men who deserved better. It is doubtful, though, that these leaflets had any significant impact on morale. A censorship report on Canadian Army mail quotes a letter on this subject: 'The Germans dropped some leaflets to show what happened to our guys over there. I wonder if they think that we imagine we are on a picnic? We know what is to happen when there is a war on, and they will never scare us with pictures.'

The British military 'spin doctors' also went into action after the raid. A Combined Operations file concerning 'public relations' contains a 'News Guidance' memo for internal circulation, which stated: 'in spite of still [*sic*] opposition [which was fully anticipated], the raid achieved its basic purpose, namely the successful landing of troops and tanks on a heavily defended beach. The total casualties suffered by the forces involved in the operation was not more than 30%.'

These claims were somewhat misleading: the 30 per cent casualties figure glossed over the extent of the carnage among those who had gone ashore. The Combined Report gave the proportion of casualties to troops engaged among the Canadian 2nd Division, Nos 3, 4, 6 and 10 Commandos, the Royal Marine Commando and United States Rangers as 59.5 per cent, and for the Canadian Forces the figure was 68 per cent.

The lessons learned

The archives contain a great deal of material concerning the lessons learned from the Dieppe Raid. The chief one referred to was that a strongly defended port could be successfully seized by a frontal assault without intense preliminary bombing and fire from warships. Earl Mountbatten made this point in a television interview for Canadian broadcasting on 9 September 1962, and went on to explain that the germ of the idea of 'Mulberry harbours' – prefabricated mobile harbours used during the invasion of Normandy in 1944 – came out of the experience of Dieppe. He referred to the 'Mulberry' as a means of bringing 'our own port with us.' Mountbatten also maintained that 'the Germans misread the lessons of Dieppe' and went on strengthening their port defences and garrisons as their top priority, rather than paying more attention to their beaches.

Other lessons learned in the Combined Report on the raid included the need for greater flexibility in the operation plan, for closer integration between the services, for fire support, and for better support craft.

In his television interview, Mountbatten summed up as follows: 'The Duke of Wellington is credited with having said that the battle of Waterloo was won on the playing fields of Eton. I have no doubt that the battle of Normandy was won on the beaches of Dieppe. For every one man who died at Dieppe in 1942, at least ten or more must have been spared in Normandy in 1944.'

Controversy

Some historians, notably Professor Brian Villa, have focused on the decision to relaunch the operation, and have made the argument that Mountbatten did not seek proper permission for this, pointing to the lack of a clear record of approval for Operation *Jubilee* from the chiefs-of-staff. However, Mountbatten always maintained that the decision to remount the operation was done 'in circumstances of quite unusual secrecy' (for security reasons), and so nothing was put on paper at the meeting of the chiefs-of-staff.

Churchill's note to Gen Hastings Ismay, 21 December 1942. ▼

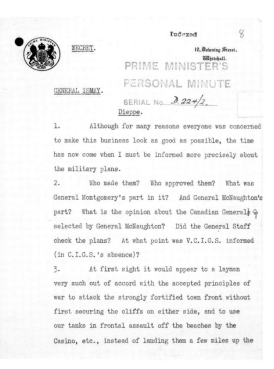

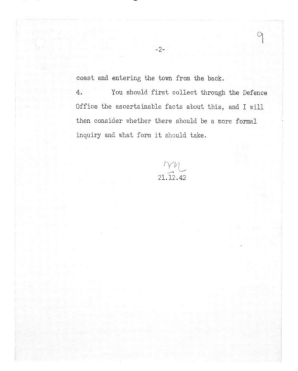

In a speech on 8 September 1942, Churchill told the House of Commons: 'I, personally, regard the Dieppe assault, to which I gave my sanction, as an indispensable preliminary to full-scale operations.'

In private, Churchill was clearly disturbed by the outcome of Dieppe, as can be seen by his personal note to Gen Hastings Ismay of the War Cabinet, dated 21 December 1942. The forceful and direct tone of this note is striking. Ismay replied with reference to the Combined Report on the operation and Churchill did not pursue the issues further at this time.

The Dieppe Raid was a tragedy of war, but the summing-up in the official *History of the Combined Operations Organisation 1940–1945* still retains validity: 'Dieppe was a landmark in the history of combined operations which makes a fitting climax to the story of Raiding. A raid on a considerable scale had been planned, mounted and executed against severe opposition.'

Combined Operations went on to participate in Operation *Torch*, the British–US invasion of French North Africa in November 1942; and Operation *Husky* (see page 197), the Allied invasion of Sicily in July–August 1943. After Sicily, Combined Operations launched assaults at Salerno and Anzio in the Mediterranean, and gave major assistance with planning and training for Operation *Overlord*, the Allied invasion of north-west Europe that took place in June 1944. There is no doubt that Combined Operations Command made a huge contribution towards the winning of the war.

OPERATION *VP 101 (BARBARA)*
The plan to sabotage the dock at Bergen, 1943

At the end of November 1943, an audacious raid was made against the German-occupied port of Bergen. The intention was to place explosive charges under the Laksevaag floating dock that supported the Bergen-based U-boats and German ships in the harbour.

The craft
This was the first and only operational use of Welman craft. These were basically one-man-operated submersibles that could carry a removable warhead. According to a wartime report, 'the operator sat in comparative comfort in the dry, with warm hands and feet and could take food, with the

Below and overleaf) photographs from a British intelligence report on Bergen from November 1943 showing the Laksevaag target area with one of the floating docks. ▼

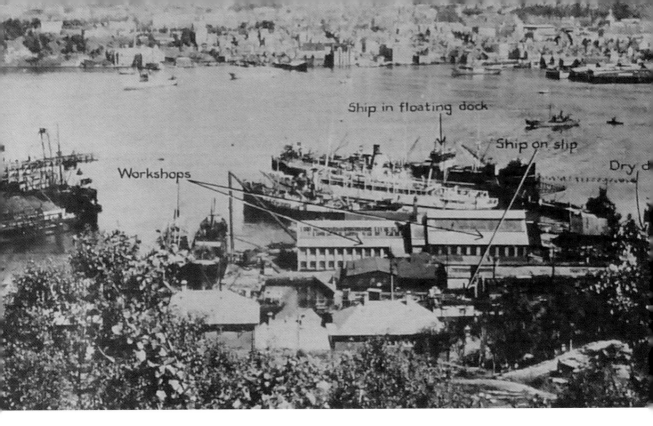

Ship in floating dock

Ship on slip

Workshops

Dry d

knowledge that if necessary, the craft could be surfaced and the hatch opened eliminating any fear of claustrophobia.'

MOST SECRET

◀ Among the locations in which Welman submersibles were tested was the Queen Mary reservoir at Staines, Surrey.

A Welman during early trials.

With an explosive charge attached, they measured just over 20ft long, with a hull diameter of just over 2½ft. Their range was about 30 miles at a maximum speed of around 4 knots, and they could safely dive to 100ft, allowing them to pass under torpedo nets. If necessary, they could stay submerged for some ten hours.

However, one big problem with the design was that they had no periscope. So, to assist with navigation, the craft were fitted with a gyro-compass that was accurate to 10 degrees per hour. Without a periscope, it was necessary for the craft to surface so that the operator could find his bearings through the windscreen and four portholes, or simply open the hatch and look out.

The basic design for the Welman originated from the aptly named Col John Dolphin of the Royal Engineers in mid-1942, and was developed in association with Special Operations Executive's Professor Dudley Newitt. The idea was that the Welman would be carried by a submarine or flying boat to within 20 miles of its target, before being released to stealthily make its attack, attaching its time-delayed explosive charge to the hull of a ship before escaping undetected.

Three prototypes went into development at SOE's Station IX, a highly secret facility not far from the town of Welwyn, just north of London; thus the craft was called a Welman (Welwyn One-Man Submarine).

A number of other submersibles were also being developed around the same time, including Chariots, which required operators to sit in diving suits 'on' the craft, rather than 'in it'; and Welfreighters, which were bigger than Welmans and could carry three men inside. There were also the larger three- or four-man X-craft and the very much smaller single-man 'Sleeping Beauties' (submersible canoes capable of diving to 40ft). The disadvantage of all these other craft was that they required a bit more training before they could be used. Furthermore, the Welman was generally cheaper and easier to produce than many of the other submersibles.

The plan

The theory of the proposed raid had been tested during trials, when a Welman successfully got past anti-submarine protection, including nets, and placed a dummy charge on HMS *Howe*. Mock attacks were also practised against HMS *Titania*, with a dummy charge being successfully placed beneath her.

The 30th Flotilla, manned by officers and men of the Royal Norwegian Navy, were already operating from the Shetlands using motor torpedo boats (MTB) to attack targets in Scandinavian waters, and they agreed to be the first to try the Welmans, with Bergen as the target.

Prior to the Bergen operation, Welmans had successfully undertaken a practice attack on HMS *Howe*, seen here en route to the Suez Canal.

An intelligence report on the port dated 1 November 1943 states that until June 1941, there was only one 500ft-long floating dock at Bergen, which was moored off the end of the jetty at Laksevaag. However, with the development of the U-boat facilities there, more floating docks were provided; as of November 1943, it was reported that there were three 270ft-long and two 350ft-long floating docks in the area.

On 20 November 1943, MTB *635* and MTB *625* left Lunna Voe, Shetland, carrying four Welmans to be used in the raid. The four men undertaking this dangerous mission were Lt Carsten Johnsen of the Royal Norwegian Navy, Lt Bjørn Pedersen of the Norwegian Army, Lt Basil Marris of the Royal Navy Volunteer Reserve, and Lt James Holmes of the Royal Navy.

Preparing for the mission

In training, Pedersen had a lucky escape when his craft experienced technical problems and sank in 180ft of water. He escaped and ascended to the surface without any form of breathing apparatus, and was dragged from the water unconscious with blood coming out of his ears, nose and mouth. Fortunately, he was very fit and had good medical attention that saw him recover within a few hours, at which point he apparently asked if he could have another go.

Marris also had a dangerous moment during a Welman trial while being towed at a depth of around 60ft, when water started entering his craft and it reared up vertically. Via a communications line to the surface vessel, he reported that 'his feet were getting wet'. Hauling the craft to the surface with the extra weight of water presented some difficulties and, while the recovery operation was underway, the communications line came adrift. However, once clear of the water, Marris was able to get out. It was reported that he 'had his nerves well under control', although the medical officer in attendance confirmed he was suffering from shock.

The men taking part in the raid were fully aware of just how dangerous the mission would be and were each issued with a handgun, though it is debatable how useful these might prove in the event of trouble. The main concern was simply being able to navigate without being either spotted or heard at the times when they were surfaced.

There were two ways to navigate a Welman. One was to dive the craft and work to a previously calculated formula – a method that was favoured by

◀ Before the war, Carsten Anker Johnsen had been a policeman in Bergen. He had escaped the German occupation in March 1941 and made his way to the UK, where he began his training with the Welman submersibles on 1 August 1943. He spoke German, as well as very good English.

Bjørn Pedersen was born in Bergen and had been a general clerk before the war. He came to the UK in 1940. His training with Welman craft began at the same time as Johnsen's, though he was slightly handicapped by his lack of fluent English. ▶

◀ James Francis Lind Holmes was born in Portsmouth and by the end of the war had considerable experience with small underwater craft, including Welmans, Welfreighters and Sleeping Beauties.

[Ho]ng Kong-born Basil McDonald Marris had [pr]eviously been a clerk with the Gas Light and Coke [Co]mpany. He also had good experience with small [su]bmersibles and was involved heavily in the [W]elman trials. ▷

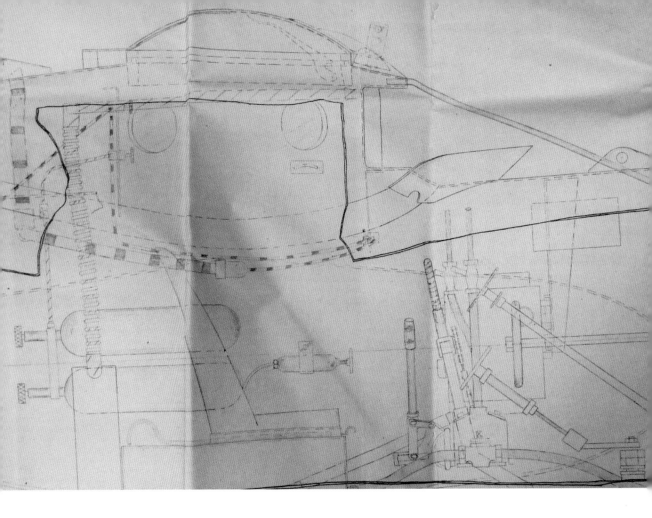

▲ Drawing showing the Welman operators' seating position and controls.

Holmes, as he did not want to be distracted by any light, landmark or other object of interest. The other method was to remain surfaced and steer via various landmarks and lights, only submerging when a threat was immediately apparent. This was the method chosen by the other three men.

The attack

As planned, the attack on Bergen progressed with the craft being launched from the MTBs at the entrance to the fjord at Solsviksund. The intention was they would make their way first to the island of Hjelthholmen, outside Bergen's heavily defended harbour. Here, they would camouflage the Welmans and remain in hiding until continuing the raid the following evening. Unfortunately, however, during the day of 21 November, there was a great deal of unexpected activity in the vicinity by Norwegian fishermen that resulted in the Welmans being discovered. It was thus feared the Germans could have received word that some sort of attack was about to happen.

Nevertheless, at approximately 18:45 that day, 2nd Lt Pedersen left Hjelthholmen in his Welman to begin his attack run. He was followed at 15-minute intervals by Lt Holmes, Lt Marris and Lt Johnsen, in that order.

The sea was calm, but fine rain and local fog hampered navigation. Fortunately, Holmes had fitted his craft with a waterproof cape that meant he could sit his Welman low in the water, presenting a smaller silhouette, but when needed he could come to full buoyancy, open the hatch all the way and stand up with a pair of binoculars.

Pedersen, taking the lead, soon observed the tail of a convoy heading into Bergen and kept to starboard of this close to land, avoiding a German watch boat that was signalling the convoy. As he rounded a projecting headland, he suddenly saw a small boat heading straight for him. He immediately dived towards the entrance to Byfjorden and proceeded for some 15 minutes submerged.

Once resurfaced, he expected to see the lights from two lighthouses, but visibility was poor due to the rain on the portholes in the Welman's small conning tower, and he could only see one light. He therefore opened the hatch and stood up to get a better view. At that moment, he saw the outline of a minesweeper some 40–60 yards away, which was signalling another vessel hundreds of yards away. The signalling immediately stopped and the light was instead directed straight at Pedersen. In a few seconds, other searchlights converged on him.

Before he could even half submerge, shots were fired from a 20mm gun that threw water up around the bows of his Welman. Knowing that the game

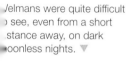

Welmans were quite difficult to see, even from a short distance away, on dark moonless nights. ▼

was up, and fearing that if he were to dive, depth charges would be dropped that could kill both him and his comrades, Pedersen stood up and surrendered, dropping all his papers over the side. Unfortunately, they did not sink and were later recovered by the Germans.

The Welman was taking in water having been hit, though Pedersen later reported that they had apparently not shot directly at him, as at such a short range they could not possibly have missed. To assist in sinking his craft, therefore, Pedersen opened the trim tank flooding valve. As a rubber dingy approached, he opened the main vent and jumped into the water.

The other Welman operators apparently heard the shooting and realized that the Germans would know an attack was in progress and make their defences ready for them. They immediately aborted the mission and turned back.

Johnsen subsequently abandoned his Welman in Hjeltefjorden, near Vindnes, and swam to the shore. Marris, who had struggled with navigating, also made for the shore, abandoning his Welman near Brattholmen. Holmes also came ashore, making his way to Sotra. Assisted by the Norwegian resistance, the three men all met up at Sordalen further up the coast.

The aftermath of the raid

Between November 1943 and February 1944, the three men remained in hiding in Norway, making one abortive attempt to reach the UK by fishing boat in late December. This failed due to extremely bad weather and the poor condition of the boat. Many attempts were also made to recover them by MTBs and submarine chasers from Shetland, but none was successful, until 5 February 1944.

Pedersen, meanwhile, having been taken aboard the minesweeper, was interrogated by the Kriegsmarine the whole night. The next morning, the Gestapo arrived and took him away for further questioning. He had been wearing a Royal Navy volunteer reserve uniform and claimed to be a British officer rather than a member of the Norwegian forces. This was a story he stuck to, as it is thought that he would probably have been executed had the Germans known his true identity.

It was acknowledged by the British authorities later that during the subsequent questioning, Pedersen displayed very marked coolness and presence of mind. He gave such answers that the Germans were completely misled as to the plan of the operation, the number of craft taking part and the arrangements made for the recovery of the officers engaged. He spent the rest of the war in a prison camp in Germany.

Although the raid had not been successful, lessons were learned. Two further submersible raids took place using X-craft, which resulted in the floating dock finally being destroyed in September 1944.

On 2 September 1949, the British Naval Attaché in Oslo contacted the Director of Naval Intelligence informing him that a Welman submarine had been recovered at Bergen. It was agreed that it would be donated to a local museum. It is James Holmes' Welman that is now on display at the Naval Museum in Horten, Norway.

OPERATION *POSTMASTER*
Hunting for U-boats off the coast of West Africa

In 1941, the British Admiralty started receiving reports that German U-boats were refuelling and making repairs in the rivers of Vichy French Africa. In response, the Small Scale Raiding Force (SSRF) was sent to investigate. Also known as No. 62 Commando, SSRF had been formed in1941 and consisted of a small group of 55 commando-trained personnel under the command of Maj Gus March-Phillipps working with SOE and under the operational control of Combined Operations Headquarters.

The SSRF's transport on raids was a 65-ton Brixham yacht trawler called *Maid Honor*, which left Poole in Dorset with a five-man crew under March-Phillipps for West Africa on 9 August 1941. The rest of the SSRF were under the command of Capt Geoffrey Appleyard and had departed earlier aboard a troop transport ship. After six weeks under sail, on 20 September 1941 *Maid Honor* arrived at Freetown, Sierra Leone – the agreed rendezvous for both groups, Appleyard's party having arrived at the end of August. The team now reunited, SSRF began combing the coastline for the U-boat refuelling bases and U-boats – to no avail.

Despite this, SOE maintained a presence in West Africa so that it could observe Vichy French, Spanish and Portuguese territories and thereby identify and hopefully hinder any activities that threatened Britain's colonial possessions. As part of this process, while searching for German submarine bases, SOE

Maj John Appleyard, January 1941. ▼

Maid Honour with Appleyard (left) Desgranes (centre) and March-Phillipps (right). ▶

apt Graham Hayes, January 942. ▶

agents became aware of three vessels in the port of Santa Isabel on the Spanish island of Fernando Po, 20 miles off the coast of Africa near the borders of Nigeria and the Guinea.

Targeting the problem

The three ships were the Italian 8,500-ton merchant vessel *Duchessa d'Aosta*, a large German tug *Likomba*, and a diesel-powered barge *Bibundi*. *Duchessa d'Aosta* had a working radio, which was considered a threat since it had the potential to enable those on board to transmit details of Allied naval or merchant shipping movements to Axis submarines or surface raiders, which could then attack and sink this shipping. Its declared cargo was: 3,000,000lb of wool; 316,610lb of hides and

◀ Customs House, Santa
Isabel harbour, Fernando Po.

skins; 1,300,000lb of tanning materials; 4,000,000lb of copra; 544,660lb of crude asbestos fibre; and more than 1,100,000 ingots of electrolytic copper. The first page of the ship's cargo manifest, however, was not presented to the port authorities and the ship's captain refused to provide them with any details, which led to speculation that the vessel was also carrying arms, ammunition or parts (chassis) for Axis military vehicles.

◀ Capt Gus March-Phillipps,
January 1942.

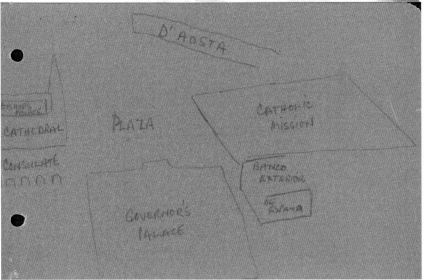

Duchessa d'Aosta in Santa
Isabel harbour, 1941. ▶

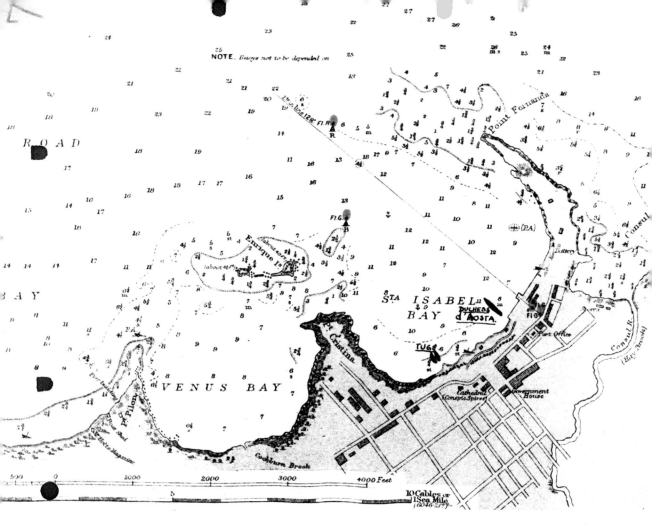

In response, during his visits to the island, SOE agent Leonard Guise kept the ships under observation, and in August 1941 provided a proposal to seize *Likomba* and disable *Duchessa d'Aosta* – approval for which was duly given by the Admiralty in November 1941.

Preparations and political problems

To transport the raiding force of four SOE agents and 11 commandos from the SSRF to the island, two tugs, *Vulcan* and *Nuneaton*, crewed by 17 men recruited from the local population, were provided by the Governor of Nigeria. However, the British General Officer Commanding (GOC) West Africa Command, Gen Sir George Giffard, refused to support the mission and would not release the 17 men required, on the grounds that it would compromise other plans and that such an act of piracy would have grave repercussions.

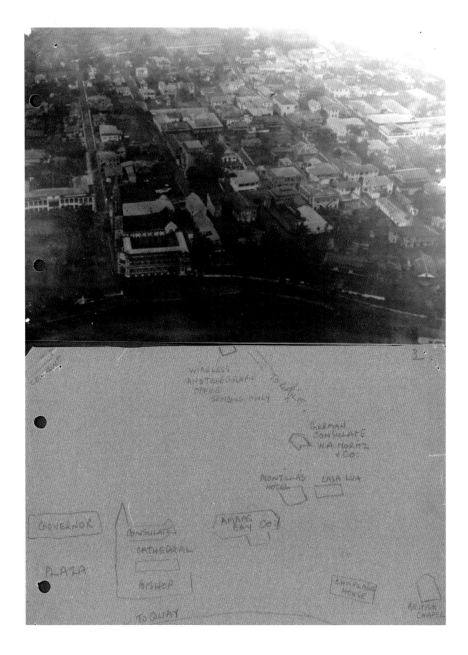

Responding to these concerns, the Admiralty suspended the operation. To make matters worse, neither the Foreign Office nor the British Embassy in Madrid were in favour of the operation – the latter due to concerns about the possible reaction of the Spanish government to such an act.

It was thus not until 6 January 1942 that SSRF finally received the go-ahead, supported by the Foreign Office, on the proviso that although suspicion of British involvement in the raid was inevitable, so long as there

was no tangible proof, this in itself would not be a problem. Moreover, once it was appreciated that Ian Fleming of Naval Intelligence (and later the author of the James Bond novels) had worked out a cover story, the Admiralty was more relaxed about the plan going ahead. As an added safeguard, the Admiralty also dispatched HMS *Violet*, a Flower class corvette, to detain the vessels at sea and support Fleming's cover story that the ships had been intercepted while heading back to Europe.

Distracting the enemy

Having been given the green light, the plan could now be put into action. The first move was for SOE agent Richard Lippett to secure a job with the shipping company John Holt & Co (Liverpool), which had business offices on the island. Having successfully taken up the post and secured employment on the island, Lippett could make preparations for the raid and keep his ear to the ground. In this manner, he became aware that the crew of *Duchessa d'Aosta* frequently accepted invitations to parties ashore and had held their own party aboard ship on 6 January 1942. By pretending to be a partygoer, Lippett then managed to gain vital insider information about the readiness of the ship for sea, crew numbers and the watch arrangements.

A few days later, on the morning of 11 January, raiders left Lagos in their two tugs and headed for Santa Isabel harbour, practising lowering folbots (folding kayaks) and boarding ships under the supervision of Capt Graham Hayes while en route. By 23:30, the tugs were in position some 200 yards outside the harbour. Ashore, Lippett had arranged for the 12 Italian officers from *Duchessa d'Aosta* and two German officers from *Likomba* to be invited to, and attend, a dinner party. Even the governor was to be distracted by means of a 'honey trap'. The stage was set.

The raid

As the tugs entered the harbour, the boarding parties assembled on the decks. *Vulcan*, with March-Phillipps and Appleyard on board, headed for *Duchessa d'Aosta*. As they drew near, they could see some men on the deck of the ship shining a light in the direction of the tug, but beyond this there was no response. Simultaneously, the folding kayaks under the command of Hayes from the tug *Nuneaton* were paddling towards *Likomba* and *Burundi*, which were moored next to each other.

When challenged by the watch on *Burundi*, the crew replied that they were bringing the ship's captain back from the dinner party ashore. The men from the canoes then boarded *Burundi* and the two-man crew on watch jumped overboard. Next, explosive charges were planted on the anchor chain and the commandos guided *Nuneaton* alongside *Likomba* so that they could carry her and *Burundi* in tow. Once everything was in place, the charges were blown and *Nuneaton* began to tow *Likomba* out of the harbour.

Meanwhile, on the *Duchessa d'Aosta*, 11 men had got aboard from *Vulcan*, and one group now planted explosive charges on the anchor chains while another searched below decks, taking the crew prisoner. They then blew the explosives on the anchor chains and *Vulcan* started to tow *Duchessa d'Aosta* out of the harbour. Having been woken by the explosions, the local population gathered on the pier for a ringside view of the ships' departure, but no one attempted to do anything to stop them, and the 6in guns protecting the harbour weren't fired at all. Instead, some of the anti-aircraft guns opened up on imaginary targets as their crews assumed that Santa Isabel was being attacked from the air! The whole mission had lasted just 30 minutes, without any casualties among the raiding teams.

On 15 January, once out at sea, March-Phillipps established watches and had guards placed on the 29 prisoners. That evening, both tugs experienced engine trouble and there were problems with the tow ropes linked to the captured vessels, but despite this, the next day, *Vulcan* managed to successfully rendezvous with and be 'captured' by HMS *Violet*. *Nuneaton*, meanwhile, managed to contact the Nigerian collier *Ilorin* by semaphore and a ship was thus sent from Lagos to tow them in.

The political consequences

Back in London, the reaction was quite positive. SOE had clearly shown its ability to plan and undertake missions regardless of the political outcome. As Hugh Dalton, Minister of Economic Warfare in charge of SOE, explained to Winston Churchill: 'other neutral governments would be impressed that Britain would if needed disregard the legal formalities of war in their efforts to succeed.' The head of SOE's Africa station opined to the head of SOE, Colin Gubbins, that: 'perhaps next time it will not be necessary for prolonged negotiations before undertaking a 30 minute operation.'

The Spanish government, as predicted, was furiously indignant about the ships' 'departures', which were seen as a breach of Spain's neutrality. Indeed, the foreign minister even went so far as to describe the operation as an attack on Spanish sovereignty, and threatened to answer it by force of arms.

In Germany, meanwhile, a radio broadcast claimed that a British warship destroyer had entered the harbour and blown up the ship's anchor cables and shot the ship's crews. After the 21 January 1942 edition of *Völkischer*

Beobachter published an article with the headline 'British Denials – Admiralty Lies on Act of Piracy', the Admiralty responded by saying:

> In view of the German allegations that Allied naval forces have executed a cutting-out operation against Axis ships in the Spanish port of Santa Isabel, Fernando Po, the British Admiralty considers it necessary to state that no British or Allied ship was in the vicinity ... As a result ... of the German Broadcast, the British Commander-in-Chief dispatched reconnaissance patrols to cover the area. A report has now been received that a large unidentified vessel has been sighted, and British naval vessels are proceeding to the spot to make investigations.
>
> The British patrols found the *Duchessa d'Aosta* in difficulties and boarded and captured the ship which was then taken to Lagos in Nigeria, arriving on 21 January 1942.

To cover up what had happened, the Foreign Office questioned why the Spanish authorities were claiming that British forces had anything to do with the departure of the vessels when there had clearly been no British warships in the area. Rather, the Spanish were told, it appeared that the crews of the vessels had become frustrated by the length of their stay in Fernando Po and with the attitude of the Spanish authorities, who seemed to be harassing men who had left the ships to go and live ashore. The crews had 'obviously' taken matters into their own hands, mutinied and sailed the vessels out of Santa Isabel harbour and then, without the guidance of their officers, encountered difficulties in controlling the vessels once at sea. It was at this point, the story went, that British patrol ships had come upon the Axis vessels, boarded them and sailed them to the nearest British port.

apt Richard Lippett, January 942.

The aftermath

Richard Lippett, who had remained on Fernando Po, was taken in for questioning by the Spanish, whom he persuaded that he had had nothing to do with the departure of the ships and had not spent any money on the party for the ships' officers. He was duly released, but was refused permission to leave the island. He finally managed to escape secretly by canoe, arriving in British territory on 1 March 1942.

In recognition of their roles in the operation, March-Phillipps was awarded the Distinguished Service Order; Hayes was awarded the Military Cross; Appleyard receive a Bar to his Military Cross; and Lippett and Guise were each awarded Membership of the Order of the British Empire. The only professional sailor and the team's 'hunter-killer' on the raid, Private Anders Lassen, was given the commission of lieutenant and awarded the Military Cross. Sadly, March-Phillipps, Hayes, Appleyard and Lassen were all killed on active service during or after undertaking other raids or missions later in the war.

▲ Maj Anders Lassen, January 1942.

As for the ships, *Maid Honor* was left in Lagos and eventually sold to the Sierra Leone government as a trawler; *Duchessa d'Aosta* was sailed to Greenock, in Scotland, and then managed by the Canadian Pacific line as the *Empire Yukon* for the Ministry of War Transport; and *Likomba* was managed by the Elder Dempster Lines, who renamed it *Malakel* in 1947 and sold it to Liberia in 1948.

OPERATION *ANTHROPOID*
The assassination of Reinhard Heydrich, 1942

Reinhard Heydrich, dressed for fencing, 1942. ▼

Operation *Anthropoid* was the code name for the assassination of General of Police, SS Gen Reinhard Heydrich, head of the Reich Security Main Office (RSHA or *Reichssicherheitshauptamt*) from September 1939, and acting *Reichsprotektor* of the Protectorate of Bohemia and Moravia in Czechoslovakia from September 1941.

One of the key figures involved with the rise to power of Adolf Hitler, Heydrich wielded tremendous authority and carried out many nefarious tasks during the war, not least spearheading Operation *Reinhard*, the so-called Final Solution or Holocaust of the Jews in Europe.

At the time of Heydrich's second appointment, as acting *Reichsprotektor*, Hitler wanted an end to any softness of approach towards the Czechs: a weakness that appeared to him to encourage both anti-German sentiment and resistance in the form of strikes and sabotage. Heydrich – a brutal, arrogant man who liked to demonstrate his contempt for the resistance forces and his faith in the Nazi security forces by driving with his chauffeur in an open-topped Mercedes – seemed just the man for the job.

The aims of the mission

Meanwhile, in London, the Czech government-in-exile under Edvard Beneš was under mounting criticism from the British because they felt that the Czechs had carried out very little in the way of resistance activity since the occupation began – something that the Czechs attributed to the fierceness of the Nazi occupation.

The government-in-exile therefore decided that executing Heydrich in retribution for his crimes against humanity would send a strong message to the Nazis that they were not beyond the vengeance of the Allies and the local resistance, and hoped that meting out justice on the murderous Protector would both inspire and unite the Czech and Slovak populations against the Nazis.

The operation was initiated by František Moravec, head of Czech intelligence, who briefed Brig Colin Gubbins, Director of Operations of SOE. Gubbins gave his support. Knowledge of the operation – code named *Anthropoid* – was strictly limited within SOE.

Preparing for the mission

Preparations began on 20 October 1941. Moravec had selected 24 of the best Czech soldiers based in Britain, who then went to one of SOE's commando training centres at Arisaig in Scotland for further training and assessment. From among the men, WO Jozef Gabcik (Slovak) and Staff Sgt Karel Svoboda (Czech) were initially chosen to carry out the operation on 28 October 1941 (Czechoslovakia's Independence Day), but having received a head injury during training, Svoboda had to be replaced by Jan Kubiš (Czech). This caused delays in the mission while false documents were prepared for Kubiš and he completed his training, which included a day's training on unarmed and close-quarters knife combat with SOE's legendary martial skills trainer William Ewart Fairbairn at Station 17, Brickendonbury Manor, Hertfordshire.

When Kubiš was finally ready, Gabčík, Kubiš and seven other Czech soldiers in two teams – named Silver A and Silver B (each with separate objectives) – were flown from RAF Tangmere by a Halifax of No. 138 Squadron RAF on 28 December 1941. Although the plan was that they would land near Pilsen, due to navigation problems they in fact landed near Nehvizdy, east of Prague and had then to get to Pilsen to contact their Czech helpers.

Once they reached Prague, they contacted families and resistance groups who would help them prepare for the operation – something that the resistance leaders, fearful of the reprisals, begged the government-in-exile not to do. Beneš was having none of it, however, and the team set to working out a strategy. The initial plan was that they would kill Heydrich on a train, but they quickly realized that this wasn't possible. Another was to kill him on a forest road that led from Heydrich's home to Prague, and a third – the one they opted for – was to kill him in Prague itself.

The attack

At 10:30 on 27 May 1942, Heydrich began his daily journey from his home in Panenské Břežany to his HQ at Prague Castle, driven by his usual driver, Klein. Little did he know that Gabčík and Kubiš were lying in wait at a tram stop positioned on a sharp bend in the road near Bulovka Hospital in Prague, where the car would be forced to slow down. Josef Valcík, meanwhile, was positioned about 100 yards north to act as a spotter.

As Heydrich's open-topped Mercedes 320 Convertible B reached the curve, Gabčík stepped out and tried to open fire with his Sten submachine gun, but at the critical moment it jammed. Heydrich, rather than driving off, then ordered Klein to stop, whereupon he stood up to try to shoot at Gabčík. Kubiš now threw a modified anti-tank grenade concealed in a briefcase at the car, the blast from the explosion tearing through the vehicle, carrying shrapnel and fibres from the upholstery and forcing them into Heydrich's body, and also injuring Kubiš. Gabčík and Kubiš, somewhat stunned from the explosion themselves, then fired at Heydrich but didn't manage to hit him. Heydrich staggered out of the car, returning fire, and tried to chase Gabčík, but collapsed.

It was at this point that the driver, Klein, returned from his abortive attempt to chase Kubiš, who had fled the scene by bicycle. Now bleeding badly, Heydrich ordered Klein to chase Gabčík on foot, which Klein did, chasing him into a butcher's shop, where Gabčík shot him twice with a pistol before escaping to a local safe house. Gabčík and Kubiš, meanwhile, did not know that Heydrich had been seriously wounded and thought that the attack had failed.

Heydrich's injuries

Back on the road, a Czech woman and an off-duty policeman who had arrived on the scene flagged down a passing delivery van, which took

Heydrich to Bulovka Hospital. He had severe injuries to his left side, with major damage to his diaphragm, spleen and lung. A doctor packed the chest wound, while another unsuccessfully tried to remove the shrapnel splinters. A team of doctors then operated on Heydrich, reinflating the collapsed left lung, removing the tip of the fractured 11th rib, stitching the torn diaphragm, inserting several catheters and removing the spleen, which contained a grenade fragment and pieces of upholstery. That evening, Himmler's personal physician, Karl Gebhardt, arrived and administered large amounts of morphine, and thereafter Heydrich was entirely in the care of SS physicians.

Cause of death

There are contradictory accounts surrounding what actually killed Heydrich, but we do know that soon after the operation he developed a high temperature and issues with wound drainage. Despite this, after seven days, his condition appeared to be improving, until he suddenly collapsed and went into shock. He spent most of his remaining hours in a coma and died around 04:30 on 4 June. Himmler's physicians officially described the cause of death as septicemia.

One theory was that material from the car's upholstery, forced into his body by the blast of the grenade, had caused a body-wide infection. Another was that he died of a massive pulmonary embolism. In support of the latter, particles of fat and blood clots were found during the autopsy in the right ventricle and pulmonary artery, and severe oedema was noted in the upper lobes of the lungs, while the lower lobes were collapsed.

It has also been claimed that Heydrich died from botulism (botulinum poisoning) and that the anti-tank grenade used in the attack had been modified to contain botulinum toxin. However, it is perhaps unlikely that the toxin would

The gun and the hat of Reinhard Heydrich. ▼

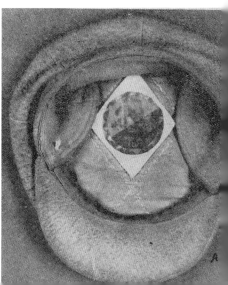

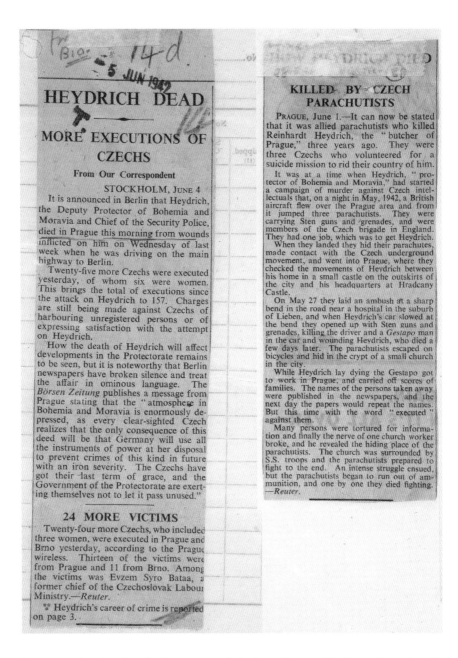

Bio. 14 d.
5 JUN 1942

HEYDRICH DEAD

MORE EXECUTIONS OF CZECHS

From Our Correspondent

STOCKHOLM, JUNE 4

It is announced in Berlin that Heydrich, the Deputy Protector of Bohemia and Moravia and Chief of the Security Police, died in Prague this morning from wounds inflicted on him on Wednesday of last week when he was driving on the main highway to Berlin.

Twenty-five more Czechs were executed yesterday, of whom six were women. This brings the total of executions since the attack on Heydrich to 157. Charges are still being made against Czechs of harbouring unregistered persons or of expressing satisfaction with the attempt on Heydrich.

How the death of Heydrich will affect developments in the Protectorate remains to be seen, but it is noteworthy that Berlin newspapers have broken silence and treat the affair in ominous language. The *Börsen Zeitung* publishes a message from Prague stating that the "atmosphere in Bohemia and Moravia is enormously depressed, as every clear-sighted Czech realizes that the only consequence of this deed will be that Germany will use all the instruments of power at her disposal to prevent crimes of this kind in future with an iron severity. The Czechs have got their last term of grace, and the Government of the Protectorate are exerting themselves not to let it pass unused."

24 MORE VICTIMS

Twenty-four more Czechs, who included three women, were executed in Prague and Brno yesterday, according to the Prague wireless. Thirteen of the victims were from Prague and 11 from Brno. Among the victims was Evzem Syro Bataa, a former chief of the Czechoslovak Labour Ministry.—*Reuter.*

* Heydrich's career of crime is reported on page 3.

KILLED BY CZECH PARACHUTISTS

PRAGUE, June 1.—It can now be stated that it was allied parachutists who killed Reinhardt Heydrich, the "butcher of Prague," three years ago. They were three Czechs who volunteered for a suicide mission to rid their country of him.

It was at a time when Heydrich, "protector of Bohemia and Moravia," had started a campaign of murder against Czech intellectuals that, on a night in May, 1942, a British aircraft flew over the Prague area and from it jumped three parachutists. They were carrying Sten guns and grenades, and were members of the Czech brigade in England. They had one job, which was to get Heydrich.

When they landed they hid their parachutes, made contact with the Czech underground movement, and went into Prague, where they checked the movements of Heydrich between his home in a small castle on the outskirts of the city and his headquarters at Hradcany Castle.

On May 27 they laid an ambush at a sharp bend in the road near a hospital in the suburb of Lieben, and when Heydrich's car slowed at the bend they opened up with Sten guns and grenades, killing the driver and a *Gestapo* man in the car and wounding Heydrich, who died a few days later. The parachutists escaped on bicycles and hid in the crypt of a small church in the city.

While Heydrich lay dying the Gestapo got to work in Prague, and carried off scores of families. The names of the persons taken away were published in the newspapers, and the next day the papers would repeat the names. But this time with the word "executed" against them.

Many persons were tortured for information and finally the nerve of one church worker broke, and he revealed the hiding place of the parachutists. The church was surrounded by S.S. troops and the parachutists prepared to fight to the end. An intense struggle ensued, but the parachutists began to run out of ammunition, and one by one they died fighting.—*Reuter.*

have remained active for long enough to have been effective, although with insufficient evidence, no conclusions can be absolute. It is certainly curious that Heydrich's post-mortem showed none of the usual signs of septicemia, although infection of the wound and areas surrounding the lungs and heart was reported. A German wartime report on the incident stated: 'Death occurred as a consequence of lesions in the vital parenchymatous organs caused by bacteria and possibly by poisons carried into them by bomb splinters.'

◀ More press cuttings reporting Heydrich's death, *Die Deutsche Polizei*, June 1942.

Bloody reprisals

Retaliation was swift, and severe: Hitler ordered an immediate investigation and suggested that Himmler send SS Gen Erich von dem Bach-Zelewski – a man who according to witnesses was even harsher than Heydrich – to Prague to mete out justice. More than 13,000 Czechs, including the relatives of Jan Kubiš and Josef Valčík and their fellows, and the families of anyone thought to have been connected with the assassination, were duly arrested. Of these, 294 people were executed in Mauthausen–Gusen concentration

126.
TASS IN ENGLISH 1543   1.6.42   HEYDRICH (dead)
HEYDRICH: ' THUNDERBOLT TO BERLIN' STAHLHELMAND CATHOLIC ARRESTS. 14 d.

STOCHKHOLM: REPORTS RECEIVED HERE FROM BERLIN REVEAL THAT
THE ATTTEMPT ON HEYDRICH CAME THERE AS A THUNDERBOLT.   WHEN
THE NEWS REACHED BERLIN MOST OF THE HITLERITE RINGLEADERS
WERE AWAY FROM TOWN.   HIMMLER WHO WAS NOTIFIED BY TELEGRAPH,
ARRIVED FROM HOLLAND A FEW HOURS LATER BY AIR, AND GOT IN
TOUCH WITH HITLER OVER THE TELEPHONE.   SHORTLY AFTER THIS
ARRESTS COMMENCED IN BERLIN (SIC).   ACCORDING TO ' STOCKHOLMS
TIDNINGEN' CORRESPONDENT SEVERAL SCORE HOSTAGES HAVE BEEN TAKEN.
REPORTS AVAILABLE THAT SEVERAL FORMER LEADERS OF ' STEEL HELMET'
AND CATHOLICS ARE AMONG ARRESTED.   THOUGH TELEPHONE COMMUNICATION
BETWEEN BERLIN AND CAPITALS OF OTHER COUNTRIES OFFICIALLY WAS
NOT SUSPENDED, IT WAS PRACTICALLY IMPOSSIBLE TO PUT THROUGH
A CALL ABRAOD ON 28TH AND 29TH MAY.
++++++1707++++++   1.6.42

/82.
U R G E N T
PRAGUE (CZECH HOME STATION) IN CZECH FOR PROTECTORATE
06.45 29.5.42   d.

HEYDRICH: CULPRITS STILL AT LARGE

YESTERDAY'S ACCOUNT OF THE ATTEMPT AGAINST HEYDRICH
(AS FLASHED) WAS REPEATED IN FULL, TOGETHER WITH THE
INSTRUCTIONS ABOUT GIVING INFORMATION LEADING TO THE APPRE-
HENSION OF THE CULPRITS.++++1002 29.5.42

▲ Reports to the Reich on the attack on Reinhard Heydrich, June 1942.

camp (262 people on 24 October 1942, 31 people on 26 January 1943 and the last one on 3 February 1944).

Tragically, this wasn't the end of the atrocities; according to one estimate, some 5,000 people in all were murdered, including many inhabitants of the village of Lidice. Here, on 9 June, as a result of faulty Nazi intelligence, the Germans committed a massacre that resulted in 199 men being killed, 195 women being deported to Ravensbrück concentration camp and 95 children being taken prisoner. Of the children, 81 were later killed in gas vans at the Chełmno extermination camp. A similar fate befell the inhabitants of the Czech village of Lezaky, where men and women alike were murdered. Both villages were then burned and the remnants of Lidice levelled.

The Czech government-in-exile had clearly not anticipated reprisals on this scale, despite the warnings they had received from the resistance leaders when they learned of the plan in Prague, or perhaps they viewed it as a price worth paying. Churchill, meanwhile, responded by suggesting that three German villages should be levelled for every Czech one that the Nazis had destroyed.

The hunt for Heydrich's executioners

In the days following the massacre at Lidice, the Nazis failed to find any leads that would help them apprehend those responsible for Heydrich's death. A deadline was therefore publicly issued to the military and the Czechoslovakian people for the assassins to be handed over by 18 June 1942. If they were not caught by then, the Germans threatened further and more extensive reprisals, believing this pressure would be enough to draw out an informant.

The assassins, meanwhile, hid with two Prague families and later in Karel Boromejsky Church, an Orthodox church in Prague dedicated to Saints Cyril and Methodius, but time was running out. Before the 18 June deadline, Karel Čurda of the 'Out Distance' sabotage group turned himself in to the Gestapo and gave them the names of the team's local contacts for the sum of 1 million Reichsmarks.

Following this lead, 750 SS soldiers under the command of SS-Gruf Karl Fischer von Treuenfeld laid siege to the church but were unable to flush the defenders out or kill them all, though Kubiš, Adolf Opalka, and Jaroslav Svarc

▲ Rows of murdered villagers in the aftermath of the Lidice massacre, June 1942. (Keystone/Getty Images)

were killed in the prayer loft during the two-hour gun battle. (Kubiš was said to have survived the battle but to have died from his injuries shortly afterwards.) Gabčík, Josef Valcik, Josef Bublik and Jan Hruby, meanwhile, chose to commit suicide in the crypt in the face of repeated SS attacks, which involved attempts to smoke them out with tear gas and to flood the crypt using fire-engine hoses. During the violence, 14 SS soldiers were allegedly killed and 21 wounded, although the SS report cited only three dead. After the battle, Čurda came to identify the bodies of the resistance fighters, including Gabčík and Kubiš.

The Orthodox hierarchy took responsibility for sheltering the assassins, in an attempt to absorb the blame and restrict recriminations, and on 4 September 1942, after being tortured, Bishop Gorazd and the priests of the Church of Saints Cyril and Methodius, along with senior lay leaders, were

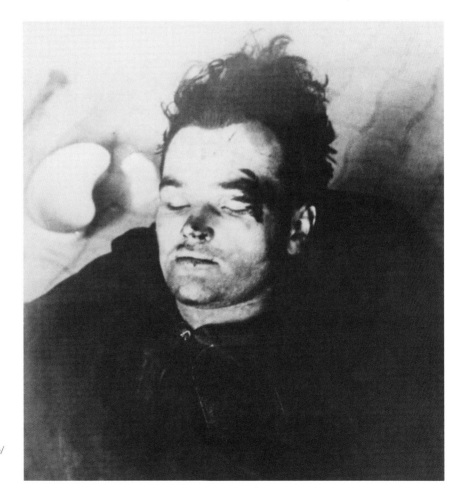

he corpse of Jan Kubiš in
e crypt of the Church of
aints Cyril and Methodius,
ne 1942. (Keystone-France/
amma-Keystone via Getty
ages) ▷

taken to Kobylisy Shooting Range in a northern suburb of Prague and shot by Nazi firing squads.

Further consequences

As if all this carnage weren't enough, there was further collateral damage. The Czech secret service had been considered one of the best, if not *the* best, agencies of its kind in occupied Europe. However, during the bloody aftermath of *Anthropoid* a notable number of its agents and circuits were caught up and killed in the broad reprisals, which seriously weakened the service's powers.

Nevertheless, the assassination did have the intended effect of inspiring the Czech and Slovak populations to further acts of resistance and defiance by showing that even leading Nazis weren't immune to the retribution and revenge of the Allies and the resistance. The assassination of Heydrich was, in fact, one of the most significant moments of the resistance in Czechoslovakia and led to the immediate dissolution of the Munich Agreement signed by the UK, France and Italy. In short, this meant that the UK and France agreed that after the Nazis were defeated, the annexed territory of the ethnic-German populated Sudetenland would be restored to Czechoslovakia.

As for Heydrich himself, two huge state funeral ceremonies were held in his honour: one in Prague for his SS rank and file, and the second in Berlin, attended by all leading Nazi figures, including Hitler.

The informant and traitor Karel Čurda was eventually caught and hanged for high treason in 1947.

Remembrance of the heroes and the victims of the Heydrich Terror

Today, there are a number of memorials for those who lost their lives in the horrifically bloody reprisals that ensued after Operation *Anthropoid*. The primary one of these, the National Memorial to the Heroes of the Heydrich Terror, lies, fittingly, beneath the Orthodox Cathedral of Saints Cyril and Methodius in Prague. There is also a memorial in Arisaig, Scotland, to the Czechoslovakian members of SOE who trained in that area, with a list of those killed and the missions in which they took part. Elsewhere, the Slovak National Museum opened an exhibition in May 2007 to commemorate the heroes of the Czech and Slovak resistance, whose actions represented one of the most important resistance actions in the whole of German-occupied Europe.

OPERATION *HARLING*

Railway sabotage in central Greece, 1942

The aim of Operation *Harling*, conceived by Col Eddie Myers and carried out on 25 November 1942 by a party of British SOE agents in cooperation with some 150 Greek partisans, was to destroy the Gorgopotamos Viaduct in central Greece in order to cut off the enemy-controlled route linking Thessaloniki and Athens. Daring in nature given how heavily defended the viaduct was, it represented one of the first major sabotage acts in Axis-occupied Europe, and the beginning of ongoing British work with and support for the Greek resistance movements ELAS and EDES.

The Simplon-Orient Express on the Gorgopotamos Viaduct, 1939–44. ▼

The targets

Operation *Harling* was devised in late summer 1942 with the objective of halting or at least slowing the passage of supplies through Greece to the German forces under FM Erwin Rommel in North Africa. The Cairo office of SOE therefore decided to send a sabotage team under the command of Lt Col Edmund Charles Wolf 'Eddie' Myers of the Royal Engineers, and his second-in-command, Maj Chris Woodhouse, to 'cut' (i.e. blow up) the railway line connecting Athens with Thessaloniki. Three viaducts in the Brallos area were targeted – the Gorgopotamos, Asopos and Papadia bridges – with the Asopos Viaduct being the priority, since it would take longer to rebuild, although the choice was to be left to the mission's leader.

A further likely goal, in retrospect, was for SOE to make contact and strike up working relations with the main Greek resistance movements and initiate a mutually beneficial partnership for the future.

The Greek resistance

Although initial attempts at armed resistance in Greek Macedonia had been quashed in the summer of 1941 by the Germans and Bulgarians, the spring and summer of 1942 saw renewed attempts, and the emergence of the first armed guerrilla units in the mountainous inner areas of central Greece and Epirus. The largest of these was the Greek People's Liberation Army (ELAS), founded by the Communist-led National Liberation Front (EAM) and led by Aris Velouchiotis.

As a young man, Velouchiotis had been active in the EAM and during the pre-war Metaxas dictatorship, had been arrested and imprisoned. However, during his trial, he had managed to escape and joined the then illegal Communist Party of Greece (KKE). Arrested again in 1939, this time he was imprisoned on Corfu, where he was forced to denounce the KKE. During World War II he served as an artillery corporal in the Greek Army on the Albanian front (1940–41) and against the Italian and then German armies until the surrender and occupation of Greece.

The second-largest resistance force was the National Republican Greek League (EDES), which was founded in September 1941, a few months after the start of the Axis Occupation. Headed by Col Napoleon Zervas, the goals of EDES were to fight the Germans and Italians, abolish the monarchy and establish a broadly social-democratic republic. A few months later, Zervas went on to found the military branch of EDES, the EOEA (National Groups of Greek Guerrillas), the activities of which were largely confined to Epirus but with some control of Aetolia-Acarnania, in the Valtos region.

Hoping to take advantage of both organizations, the British General Headquarters of the Middle East proclaimed both to be Allied armies combatant forces, with little understanding of either the precise nature, strength and political affiliation of the emerging resistance groups, or of the conditions on the ground in occupied Greece.

The SOE team

The SOE team consisted of three groups of four men: a leader, an interpreter, a sapper-cum-explosives expert and a radio operator. The first group comprised Lt Col Eddie Myers, Capt Denys Hamson, Capt Tom Barnes and Sgts Len Willmott and Frank Hernen; the second one consisted of Maj Chris Woodhouse, 2nd Lt Themis Marinos, Lt Inder Gill and Sgt Doug Phillips; and the third group consisted of Maj John Cooke, Capt Nat Barker, Capt Arthur Edmonds and Sgt Mike Chittis.

The team was flown to Greece in three B-24 Liberator planes, with some difficulty. As a result of the signal fires on the ground not being lit, the first attempt to drop the men on 28 November failed, and, although during the next attempt on 30 September the fires were lit, only two out of the three planes spotted them and successfully managed to drop their teams near Mount Giona in central Greece. The third plane, meanwhile, dropped its team – Cooke's party – near the well-guarded garrison town of Karpenissi. One unfortunate member landed inside the town itself and had to be hidden by local Greeks before making his way with the rest of his group to the hills.

Here, the party had to evade the Italian troops searching for them and at the same time find the resistance groups. This they did, connecting with the guerrillas of Aris Velouchiotis, who were less than friendly; in fact, so suspicious was Velouchiotis of the group that they were very nearly summarily executed, and had it not been for the intervention of local villagers, they would have been shot as spies of the King.

Meanwhile, the other two groups were aided by local Greeks, who concealed them in their houses and constantly moved them around to prevent their capture by Italian troops. Going their separate ways, Woodhouse set out to the town of Amfissa to establish contact with Cairo while Myers

◀ Greek Andarte girls, Mount Olympus, 1944.

and Hamson, led by a local Greek guide, undertook a reconnaissance of the putative targets. They eventually chose Gorgopotamos because it seemed to offer the best prospect of success, having just a small garrison of 80 Italians. There was also plenty of cover and both good access and a clear line of escape for the attacking force.

Contact with the resistance groups

On 2 November, Woodhouse set out once more, this time to establish contact with Zervas' EDES in the Valtos Mountains. Twelve days later, on 14 November, Maj Cooke's team rejoined the main party, bringing with them information that they had made contact with Aris Velouchiotis. Woodhouse returned on the same day, along with Zervas and 45 of his men. Zervas was immediately enthusiastic about the mission, but Velouchiotis was less keen. This was because the Athens leadership of EAM-ELAS didn't yet appreciate the potential of rural guerrilla warfare, and preferred to focus on the cities and towns. Finally, however, Velouchiotis decided to take the initiative and disobey instructions received from EAM, and agreed to join in with the mission.

The attack

The forces supporting the operation consisted of 150 men. In addition to the 12 British agents there were 86 men from ELAS and 52 from EDES. These latter forces would provide covering fire for the withdrawal and take on the garrison. The plan was for the attack to begin at 23:00 on 25 November, whereupon two small teams of eight guerrillas would cut the

en Zervas, commander of
e EDES guerrillas in Greece,
44. ▷

railway and telephone lines in both directions and cover the approaches to the bridge. The main force of 100 guerrillas would then take on and suppress the bridge's garrison, and only then would the British demolition groups lay the charges.

This was all very well, but in reality the attack on the garrison outposts went on far longer than planned, forcing Myers to send the demolition teams in to set the charges while the fighting was still going on. Critically, the setting of the charges was also held up because the girders that had to be destroyed in order to disable the bridge turned out to be a different shape from that envisaged. The engineers therefore had to dismantle the explosive packs and then recut and refit their plastic explosive charges.

Despite this difficulty, the charges were finally set and the fuses activated. The first explosion occurred at 01:30, crippling the central pier and causing two spans to collapse. The demolition teams then turned their attention to the second pier and remaining spans, setting new charges, which exploded at 02:21. Meanwhile, the ELAS outposts halted a troop train and engaged the Italian reinforcements who had been sent to back up the bridge garrison. This, too, was successful, and by 04:30 the entire attack force had successfully disengaged and retired to its assembly area, suffering only four wounded casualties.

The results

The mission was heralded a major success and key milestone for SOE, being the biggest sabotage operation carried out at that time. Although it is true that the original military objective (the disruption of supplies for FM Rommel's Afrika Korps) had been overtaken by the Allied victory at El Alamein and further advance, the success of the operation really did highlight the potential for major guerrilla actions in Axis-occupied territory in support of Allied strategic objectives. This in turn encouraged support for SOE to help develop, train and equip further resistance movements and to involve them in future strategic operations. What's more, the operation provided a massive boost for Greek morale and especially for the ELAS and EDES resistance movements, as well as for SOE, its agents and the general public, who eagerly awaited news of further victories against the Axis Powers.

In the context of this aftermath, the *Harling* mission was not completely withdrawn, as originally envisaged. Instead, while Myers and most of the

British team were evacuated, never to return to Greece, Woodhouse, Greek 2nd Lt Themis Marinos and two radio operators remained in the country in order to establish a British military mission with the newly formed Greek resistance movement. It did this to the best of its ability, but was clearly overtaken by events – namely the clashes between the resistance groups that ultimately led to the 1946–49 Greek Civil War.

Woodhouse later claimed that the success that the *Harling* team had had in 1942 in gaining the cooperation of both ELAS and EDES was due to the fact that he and Myers had worked together on this with others, and that the only way the mission would have stood a chance of alleviating the internal Greek conflict would have been for them to persuade the two groups to work together again. As it was, *Harling* was the last time that ELAS and EDES cooperated militarily. In less than a month's time, the first clashes took place between these guerrilla forces and a new chapter in Greek history began.

OPERATIONS *GROUSE/SWALLOW*, *FRESHMAN* AND *GUNNERSIDE*
The battle for heavy water, 1942–43

Operations *Grouse* (later referred to as *Swallow*), *Freshman* and *Gunnerside* were conducted by SOE in Norway in 1942 and 1943 and were at the heart of the battle for a rare commodity: heavy water (deuterium oxide).

Carrying heavy water in France

To understand the operations, we have to go back to 1939. At the time, French scientist Frédéric Joliot-Curie and his team were working in Paris,

Aerial views of the Norsk
Hydro plant in Vemork,
Norway, 1930s. ▷

racing against time to develop a nuclear bomb. Heavy water was essential to their experiments. In the same year, it became apparent that the Germans were trying to get hold of the heavy water produced in Norway by the Norsk Hydro-Elektrisk Kvaelstofaktieselskab factory (Norsk Hydro for short) in Vemork, about 65 miles west of Oslo – presumably to the same end.

Having learned of the Germans' activities, French Minister of Armaments, Raoul Dautry, approached Jacques Allier – a member of the French intelligence service who before the war had worked at the Banque de Paris et des Pays-Bas, which held most of Norsk Hydro's shares – and asked him to

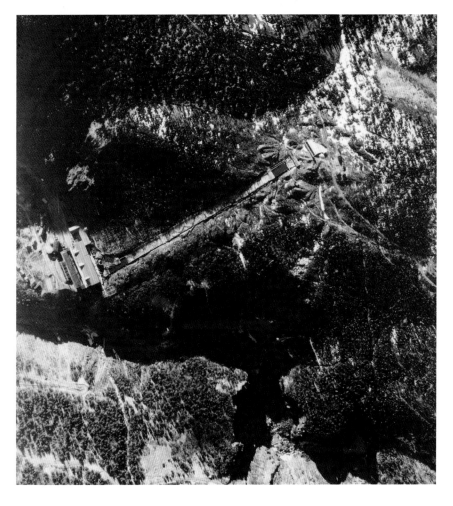

◀ Generators at the Norsk Hydro plant, 1940.

◀ Aerial photograph of the Norsk Hydro plant in daylight May 1942.

Aerial photograph of the Norsk Hydro plant at night, 1942.

negotiate with the Norwegian company to secure their entire stock of heavy water (185kg) and bring it back to France. According to a note written after the war, based on a conversation with Allier, he then 'set off for Norway with (…), as he put it, all the paraphernalia of the hero of a spy story with the exception of a false beard'.

The mission was a success and Allier managed to secure and transport the whole stock of heavy water to France, where it was entrusted to Joliot-Curie. A year later, however, the Germans started marching on to Paris and it now became imperative to keep the heavy water cylinders hidden. To this end, they were sent to Clermont-Ferrand, in central France, where they were kept in the vault of the French National Bank, before being again transported and hidden in a prison cell in Riom. When it became clear that France would fall, Allier enlisted inmates to carry the cylinders to his car – something that involved 'a "regrettable moment of tragi-comedy" when he had to threaten the warden with a revolver' – and left for Bordeaux. There, on 16 June 1940, he met with Joliot-Curie and two of his staff, Hans von Halban and Lew Kowarski, and asked them to accompany the precious cargo to Britain.

Joliot-Curie, however, refused to leave France, so Halban and Kowarski and the heavy water embarked without him on SS *Broompark* on 19 June. Having made it across the Channel, the two men both joined the Cavendish Laboratory in Cambridge, and were able to continue their research in Britain.

As for Allier, he was summoned by the Vichy Cabinet in August 1940, and had to confess that the heavy water had left France. This led to a rather farcical situation. The announcement provoked an argument between ministers, during which a number of rather crude insults were exchanged and he 'was treated to the spectacle of the Vichy Cabinet at play with the old marshal trying to drown the din by flapping his arms'.

The Norway problem

Although the heavy water in France had been safely removed from the Germans' grasp, there now remained the issue of the supplies in Norway. According to a report on operations carried out by SOE in Norway: 'In July 1942, it was decided to be of the highest importance that the existing stocks of "heavy water" (deuterium oxide), at the Norsk Hydro Works, Vemork, Norway, should be destroyed, together with the plant essential for its production.' The War Cabinet therefore approached Combined Operations Headquarters, and determined that a joint SOE–Combined Operations venture seemed to be the best course of action.

Operation *Grouse*

The first stage of the plan to destroy the Norsk Hydro Works was implemented in October 1942. Named Operation *Grouse*, its aim was to position an advance party of agents on the Hardanger Plateau above the Norsk Hydro plant. The party comprised four officers and NCOs of the Norwegian Independent Company – WO Jens-Anto Poulsson, WO Knut Hauglund, Sgt Arne Kjelstup and Sgt Claus Helberg – who were parachuted about 18½ miles from the Norsk Hydro plant on the very day on which the infamous *Kommandobefehl* was issued by the High Command of the German Armed Forces – a 'Commando Order' that stipulated that all saboteurs, military and civilian alike, were to be executed without trial.

After a long trek through the Norwegian wilderness, during which each man had to carry 132–154lb of equipment and endure severely restricted rations, they finally made contact with London on 9 November. 'Working at an altitude of some 1,200 metres and a temperature continually below zero centigrade', they started transmitting reports on weather conditions and on German defences in the Rjukan area, where the plant was located.

The weather turned out to be extremely changeable, but on 18 November the moon finally seemed to enter a favourable phase. Operation *Freshman* could begin.

Operation *Freshman*

On 19 November 1942, two aircraft left Scotland, each towing a glider carrying military personnel. The operation had two objectives: the destruction of existing stocks of heavy water and of at least part of the plant; and the collection of samples of the precious liquid.

The geographical location of the plant made the operation extremely hazardous, and there was also the significant issue of how to get the soldiers out of the country once their mission had been completed. Crossing the border into neutral Sweden seemed to be their safest bet, and intricate, dangerous escape routes were designed. All the men received intensive training, but the mission was without doubt incredibly challenging and required the agents to be in extraordinary physical condition and to have outstanding observation skills.

When the first aircraft-glider tandem reached Norway, the weather took a turn for the worse. This meant that they were unable to locate their target and as the towline started icing and the plane's fuel levels dropped dangerously low, the glider had to be 'released at sea'. It crashed not far from the coast. The second tandem, which had left 30 minutes after the first one, also crashed in Norway.

Tragically, all of the survivors were caught by the Germans and were subsequently tortured and executed, although details about their fate were only uncovered after the war. In recognition of their heroic attempt, a memorial stone was later erected in Stavanger.

Because of the failure of *Freshman*, the Germans were now aware that the plant was a target and increased their defences, which made life harder for the four men from Operation *Grouse* who were still in position on the ground. At this point, *Grouse* became *Swallow*, and the men 'continued their watch and signals amidst snow and ice, short of food and with failing power in their W/T set'.

Operation *Gunnerside*

A second attempt to attack the Norsk Hydro plant was made in February 1943, code named Operation *Gunnerside*. For this, Lt Joachim Rønneberg selected five specially trained Norwegian SOE personnel: Knut Haugland, Kasper Idland, Hans Storhaug, Fredrik Kayser and Birger Strømsheim, all of whom were excellent skiers. On 16 February 1943, they were parachuted

HAUGLAND, Knut Magne.
Nationality: Norwegian
Born: 23.9.17. Rjukan.
Occupation: Wireless Engineer.
Father: OLAF   (Norwegian)
Mother: GUNHILD nee VEGHEIM (Norwegian)
Parents'
  Address: Rjukan.
Last Address
  of Guest: Majorstveveien 32.
Documents: Passport 1603A/41 issued 15.10.41.
                  Legation, Stockholm.

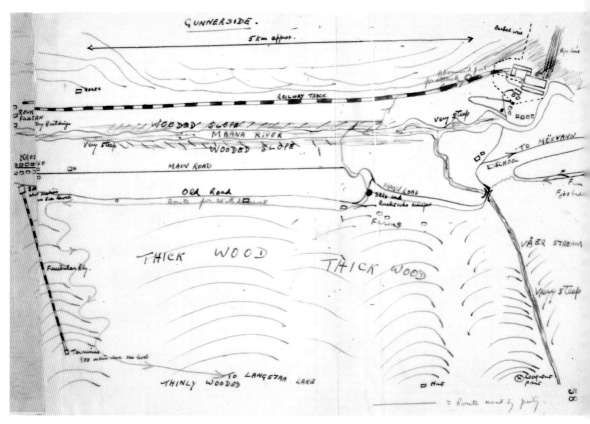

71

German anti-aircraft
efences in the area near the
orsk Hydro plant, undated.

about 18½ miles from *Swallow*'s camp and, on the evening of 23 February, after a terrible storm and a long trek, managed to rendezvous with the men from *Swallow* in a hut.

A few days later, having travelled 27 miles, the combined forces attacked the Vemork plant during the night of 27–28 February. The parties had been divided into two units: a support unit, which would neutralize the German security guards; and a demolition unit, which would place the explosive charges in the basement to destroy the production facilities. They were all wearing British uniforms as they thought that if Britain, rather than the Norwegian resistance, was blamed for the attack, the local population may escape German retaliation.

The demolition unit had planned to enter the plant through a side door, practising the manoeuvre numerous times in advance, but they hadn't anticipated that the door could be locked. Faced with this problem, Rønneberg and Kayser found an entrance tunnel and started laying out the charges, while Idland and Strømsheim, less lucky, had to break through a

Operation *Gunnerside*
ap of final approach and
thdrawal, 1942.

105

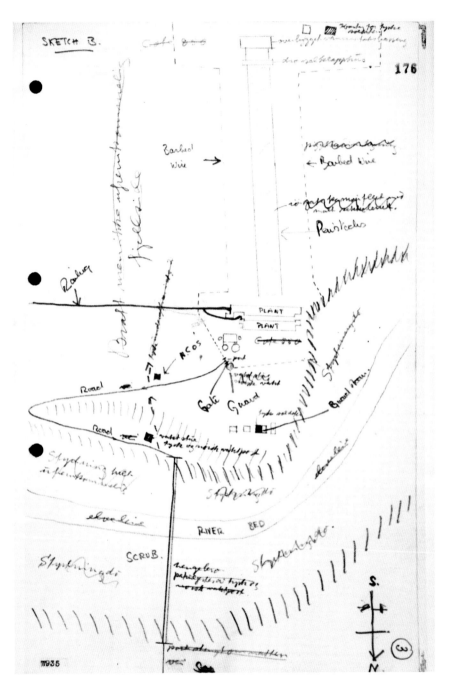

window. They had been provided with two-minute fuses, but Rønneberg decided to shorten them to 30 seconds, based on the knowledge that although doing so would make it more difficult for them to get out of the building, it would enable them to check whether they had succeeded.

The ploy worked and they all managed to get out of the room unscathed and, when they heard the muffled explosion, they knew their mission had been completed. This was confirmed in a report transmitted from Stockholm shortly after the operation, which stated:

> They came in civilian clothes to Rjukan, but when they appeared at the factory they were clad in British Uniforms and had revolvers. They told the workers in perfect Norwegian to go up in the seventh floor of the factory building where no harm would come to them. Then they went up to the vital machinery of the factory, placed their explosive charges there, pulled out the fuse and lit it. The destruction was complete as all the vital parts of the machinery were blown to pieces.

Aerial photograph of the Maan Valley and the Norsk Hydro plant, 1942.

It was estimated that the plant would be put out of action for between eight and 12 months.

After the explosion, the men regrouped outside the plant and skied towards Rjukan. Once on the plateau, the group split up again. Of the combined party of ten officers and men, five managed to cross the Swedish border after a 200-mile ski trek. The other five remained behind, including the wireless operator, who kept transmitting messages, including the report that Gen Nikolaus von Falkenhorst, the commander of German troops in Norway, had visited the plant shortly after the attack, 'which he at once ascribed to personnel from Britain' and declared it was 'the most splendid coup [he had] seen this war.'

Renewed attacks

Despite the success of Operations *Swallow* and *Gunnerside*, by August 1943, the Vemork plant had been repaired and production had started again. As it was still vital that the production of heavy water should be stopped, a choice had to be made between yet another sabotage operation and a straightforward bombing attack. The latter seemed to be the only way to ensure substantial damage, but the deputy chief of the air staff didn't think it would work; the plant was quite small and a low-level attack was impossible because of the hills surrounding it. A commando operation, on the other hand, seemed exceedingly hazardous as the Germans had substantially increased security at and around the plant since the previous attack. SOE therefore declared it was too risky to carry out another attack.

The Americans were then informed of the situation and the United States Army Air Forces (USAAF) duly attacked on 16 and 18 November 1943. Both raids were successful, and *Swallow* operatives on the ground reported on 30 November: 'Vemork completely destroyed … Will hardly be able to start production again during the war.'

On the move

Convinced that other raids would occur, the Germans decided to move the remaining stock of heavy water from Rjukan to Germany by train. Knut Haukelid, who had stayed in Norway after Operation *Gunnerside*, was ordered to stop the convoy.

Haukelid and his team of saboteurs had realized that because the Germans had considerably increased the frequency of their aerial reconnaissance missions, the only way for them to destroy the cargo was to sink the ferry transporting the train coaches across Lake Tinn, one of the deepest lakes in Europe, to the port in Skien.

Having been warned beforehand that the train would leave on 20 November, the Norwegian team broke into the ferry on the night of the 19th. They were spotted by a guard, but managed to convince him that they were workers who merely wanted to sleep on board. Having surmounted this obstacle, they successfully planted explosive charges and left the ferry undetected. At 10:30 on the morning of 20 November, DF *Hydro* sank to the bottom of the lake, which was 1,400ft deep. The battle for heavy water had been won.

The legacy

Long after the end of the war, when Joliot-Curie was not only a nuclear scientist but also 'an international communist', MI5 operatives noted that 'it [was] impossible to give in a few lines an idea of [his] scientific work'. SOE, however, did give it a good shot in 1942: the application of heavy water, they said, was 'both Churchill's and Hitler's real secret weapon and bands of scientists [were] engaged in a race for the final result.'

So, although the American raid was the *coup de grâce* for the Vemork plant, scientists such as Halban, Kowarski or Joliot-Curie couldn't have remained ahead in that race without the men involved in Operations *Grouse/Swallow*, *Freshman* and *Gunnerside*. There is also no doubt that they were the most daring operations conducted in Norway. As the Ministry of Economic Warfare put it in April 1943, 'I hope you will agree with me that the story is a particularly good one.'

THE ABDUCTION OF GENERAL KREIPE
The kidnapping of a German officer from Crete, 1944

British officers in Crete had considered the idea of capturing a senior German officer as early as 1942; travel writer and soldier Maj Patrick Leigh Fermor mentions that in November of that year Maj Xan Fielding – also a writer and SOE operative – had thought of seizing the German military governor, Alexander Andrae and later, after Andrae had been posted away, instead capturing his successor, Bruno Bräuer. As it transpired, neither of these plans were carried out, but the idea of abduction had taken root.

A practice run

Following Italy's capitulation to the Allies in September 1943, the Italian commanders on Crete, and particularly Gen Angelico Carta, became aware of the danger they were in. The Germans had ordered the Italians to concentrate their forces at certain points where they would be required to surrender all their weapons – a strategy that was not without risk. Concerned with his own well-being, Gen Carta therefore sought a private meeting with Maj Leigh-Fermor, an SOE agent who at the time played a prominent role in the Cretan resistance, to discuss the terms of his surrender to the British and, more importantly, his escape from the Greek island.

Leigh-Fermor and Carta duly came to an agreement and, according to plan, the Italian general was spirited away by boat from a remote part of the island to North Africa, together with Fermor, who briefly accompanied him.

A copycat scheme

Once in Cairo, having been made aware of the fact that the Allies had no intention of landing on Crete yet wanting to boost Cretans' morale and ridicule the Germans to boot, Leigh-Fermor and Capt William Stanley Moss came up with the idea that they could orchestrate something similar – albeit this time without the acquiescence of the hostage – in order to capture Gen Friedrich-Wilhelm Müller. Müller, the then military governor in Crete and commander of the 22nd Air Landing Division, had a reputation for brutality – he was responsible for the massacres at Viannos – and was despised by the Cretan people; he seemed the ideal target.

Having worked out the details, Leigh-Fermor duly presented the plan to his superiors, got the go-ahead (though not without some reservations), formed his team and was promoted to the rank of major. So far so good. However,

Maj Leigh-Fermor around the time of the Kreipe abduction. (Evening Standard/Getty Images) ▷

following Leigh-Fermor's return to Crete in early 1944, Müller was transferred to Hania – a major blow that could have scuppered the plan entirely. In response, rather than calling the whole thing off, Leigh-Fermor and Moss instead simply chose to target Müller's replacement in Iraklio: Gen Heinrich Kreipe.

△ Photos for an ID card for Maj Leigh-Fermor.

The new target

Gen Kreipe was a somewhat unknown quantity; nobody knew much about the German general other than that he had served during the invasion of France and on the Leningrad and Kuban fronts in Russia. What *was* known was that Kreipe took as his residence a villa in the village of Knossos – famed in Greek myth as the home of the famous labyrinth that housed the mighty Minotaur. To add to the symbolism, Kreipe's house was dubbed Villa Ariadne, named after the Cretan princess who, in legend, helped the hero Theseus find his way out of the labyrinth after slaying the Minotaur. This was all rather fitting in view of the general's well-known love for the classics.

Getting the lie of the land

On 4 February 1944, Leigh-Fermor, Moss and two Cretan SOE agents – Georgios Tyrakis and Emmanouil Paterakis – left Egypt by plane bound for Crete. Their intention was to parachute into Crete, but after arriving at the drop zone, only Leigh-Fermor was able to parachute successfully; the others had to abandon the attempt due to bad weather and were returned to Egypt. On landing, Leigh-Fermor was met by a group from the Cretan resistance, with whom he remained while Moss and the other two members of the SOE team made numerous attempts to land. Having failed three more times to get there by means of aircraft, they eventually arrived by motorboat on 4 April 1944 and were met on the beach by Leigh-Fermor and another SOE agent, Sandy Rendel.

The SOE team now also included a number of Cretans: Antonios Papaleonidas 'Wallace Beery', Michail Akoumianakis 'Mikis' and Grigorios Chnarakis. Mikis was an especially welcome addition since his house was located across the road from the Villa Ariadne. Once united, the team reconnoitred the area – an action that saw Leigh-Fermor disguise himself as a Cretan shepherd and travel on the local bus to check out the town and the area around the German headquarters. Drawing upon information gleaned during this reconnaissance, Leigh-Fermor decided that the German headquarters would be simply too difficult to penetrate.

The SOE team who captured Gen Kreipe – Moss and Leigh-Fermor are wearing German uniforms. ▼

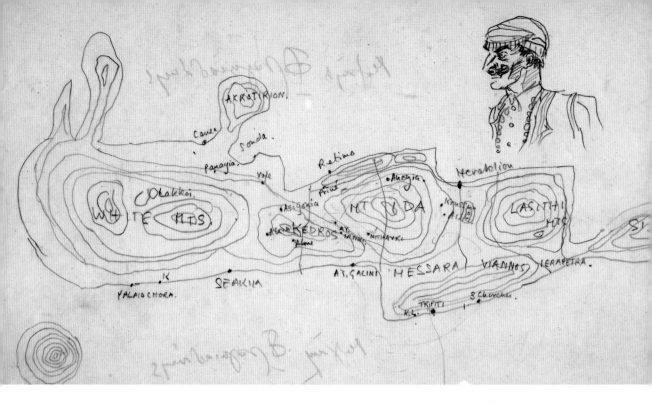

After a few days of observing the comings and goings of the general, the team finalized the details of the abduction. The plan now was for the two British officers, dressed as corporals in the *Feldgendarmerie* (German military police), to stop the general's car on his way home at what was supposed to be a routine check point. The other members of the kidnapping team were Ilias Athanasakis, Efstratios Saviolakis 'Saviolis', Dimitrios Tzatzadakis 'Tzatzas', Nikolaos Komis and Antonios Zoidakis.

The abduction

On the night of 26 April 1944, the two British officers halted the general's car before it reached the Villa Ariadne, according to plan. Once it had stopped, Leigh-Fermor and Paterakis then took care of Kreipe, while Moss struck the driver with his cosh, supported by Tyrakis. The driver, Unteroffizier (roughly, corporal) Alfred Fenske, was later found dead. In a feat of dazzling audacity, Moss next drove the team – Saviolakis, Tyrakis and Paterakis holding the general down on the back seat – in the general's car, with Leigh-Fermor impersonating the general and Moss the driver, for an hour and a half through 22 controlled roadblocks in Heraklion.

Leigh-Fermor then took the car and abandoned it, leaving in its interior documents that revealed that the kidnapping had been undertaken by British personnel supported by elements of the Greek Army, in the vain hope that no reprisals would be taken against the local population.

Moss, meanwhile, set off with the general and his Cretan escorts across country to a rendezvous where they would be joined by Leigh-Fermor. Once united, hunted by German patrols, the group moved across the mountains to reach the southern side of the island, where Maj Dennis Ciclitira had arranged for a British Motor Launch (ML 842, commanded by Brian Coleman) to pick them up.

The route across country took them over Mount Ida, in Greek mythology the birthplace of Zeus, where Kreipe is said to have recited the first line of Horace's ode 'Ad Thaliarchum' (in Latin) on seeing the white peak: 'Vides ut alta stet nive candidum Soracte' ('You see how Mount Soracte stands white with deep snow'), at which point Leigh-Fermor, a keen reader of Horace, recited the rest of the poem. Leigh-Fermor later recounted that at this point each man had realized that they had 'drunk at the same fountains' of learning.

The SOE team and the general were finally picked up from Peristeres beach near Rodakino, on the southern side of the island, on 14 May 1944. From here they were transported to safety, landing at Mersa Matruh in Egypt.

Initial German reactions

After the war, a member of Kreipe's staff reported how, on hearing the news of the kidnapping, an uneasy silence in the officers' mess in Heraklion was followed by someone saying: 'Well gentlemen, I think this calls for champagne all round.' This sentiment was not isolated; Leigh-Fermor was informed that when news of Kreipe's abduction reached the German barracks in Iraklio, many soldiers celebrated. It seems Kreipe had not been a popular commander.

Post-war correspondence explains that Kreipe was disliked by his soldiers because, among other things, he objected to the stopping of his personal vehicle for checking in compliance with his own commands concerning approved travel orders. This tension between the general and his troops in part explains why sentries at the numerous roadblocks were so cautious about stopping the general's car as Moss drove it through Heraklion.

Elsewhere, Allied propaganda efforts attempted to suggest in the immediate aftermath that the kidnapping was a cover story and that Kreipe had actually defected to the Allies, possibly fearing his own death during an Allied invasion.

Reprisals

Regardless of the general's lack of popularity, German retribution was swift and brutal: in August 1944, the village of Anogia and several villages in the Amari valley were destroyed and many Cretans massacred. In light of the fact that this sort of reaction was to be expected, many today question the wisdom of the plan. It is interesting to note, however, that the Germans did not attribute their actions to the kidnapping. Instead, a proclamation was issued with regard to the destruction of Anogia, citing the village's involvement in recent attacks on German forces, including the Damasta sabotage a few days earlier, as well as its support for the resistance and the fact that Kreipe had passed unchecked through the area.

No proclamation was made for the Amari massacres, although the German propaganda paper *Parateretis* cited the kidnapping of Kreipe as the main reason for the destruction and murder. To confuse matters further, recent contemporary Wehrmacht documents, found in the Leigh-Fermor Archive in the National Library of Scotland, describe another reason for the attacks: to suppress resistance activity, which would help the Germans to protect their flank from attack as they withdrew from Heraklion and Rethymno towards Chania along the northern coast road. There was no mention of Kreipe.

Later lives

For their part in the successful kidnapping, Maj Patrick Leigh-Fermor was awarded the Distinguished Service Order, and Capt William Stanley Moss the Military Cross, 'For [their] outstanding display of courage and audacity'. The awards were gazetted on 13 July 1944. Both went on to write and publish their own literary accounts of these events, and Leigh-Fermor became a well-respected travel writer and novelist.

Following his kidnapping, Kreipe was interrogated and then transferred to a POW camp in Canada. Later transferred to a special camp in Wales, he was released from British captivity in 1947. He met his kidnappers one more time in 1972 on a Greek TV show, and died at Northeim on 14 June 1976.

OPERATION *FOXLEY*
Taking aim at the leader: the plot to assassinate Hitler, 1944

Operation *Foxley* was an ambitious plan conceived by the SOE to assassinate Adolf Hitler and any high-ranking Nazis or members of the Führer's entourage who may be present, most likely on 13–14 July 1944, during what was to be Hitler's last visit to the *Berghof* at Obersalzberg. However, although detailed preparations were made, the operation was never carried out.

Early plans
Various schemes were considered. One of the first of these involved bombing the *Führersonderzug* 'Amerika' (in 1943 renamed 'Brandenburg') – Hitler's personal train. This seemed an obvious choice, since SOE had extensive experience of sabotage and derailing trains using high explosives. Possible locations for such an attack were the Schloss Klessheim sidings, Salzburg railway station and the routes followed by Hitler's train when travelling north to Berlin and west to Mannheim. In the end, though, the plan was dropped because Hitler's schedule was too irregular and unpredictable, with stations sometimes being informed of his arrival just a few minutes beforehand (in order to avoid just such an attack).

Another idea was to put some flavourless, lethal poison in the drinking water supply that was stored in a water tank above the Mitropa dining car on the train. This, it was proposed, could be achieved while the train was being cleaned at Salzburg station, if one of the cleaners could be induced to pour the poison into the water tank at night. This was deemed possible since the lighting at Salzburg station was extremely poor, and if there were only a couple of transport police present, these could probably be easily distracted by another agent while the deed was carried out.

Once in the tank, the strong poison solution would be mixed into the water by the movement of the train once it started moving. The key to the

◀ Document confirming
Hitler's drinking habits.

plan was the knowledge that Hitler drank a lot of tea, fruit juice and a certain amount of coffee, which would mask the presence of the poison, whereas if it were added to black tea, wines and spirits, the poison would cause cloudiness and a brown deposit, which could be noticeable.

In the end, though, this plan was considered too complicated, partly because of the need for close timing and an inside man or reliance on

The *Führersonderzug*, 1941. ▼

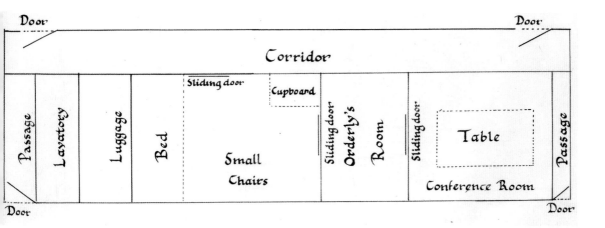

Door   Door

Corridor

Sliding door   Cupboard

Passage | Lavatory | Luggage | Bed | Small Chairs | Sliding door | Orderly's Room | Sliding door | Table / Conference Room | Passage

Door   Door

▲ Plan of Hitler's *Salonwagen* in the *Führersonderzug*.

untrained civilian personnel who had never undertaken a military or sabotage mission before. There was also no guarantee that Hitler would have a drink made with the water (if, for instance, he drank only fruit juice that day), and the risk that the poison would be detected in the tea while it was being made. Another idea was needed.

The solution: a sniper

In the end, authorities decided that a sniper attack could be the most successful method, involving fewer unpredictable variables and relying on just a couple of highly trained personnel to carry out the assassination. This covered the what. With regards to the where, the intelligence agency had received insider information in the summer of 1944 from a member of Hitler's personal guard at the Berghof who had been taken prisoner in Normandy, which revealed that while at the Berghof, Hitler routinely went for a 20-minute walk in the grounds at around 10:00, during which he was usually on his own and out of sight of sentry posts. Knowing when the Führer was in residence was easy: a swastika flag was flown from the flagpole in front of the Berghof – a clear signal that could be spotted from various locations in the nearby town, including Cafe Rottenhofer and the Doktorberg, both in Berchtesgaden. As if this weren't enough, the presence of Hitler's and other leading Nazis' special trains was another dead giveaway, as was the fact that members of the SS Führerbegleitkommando visited the local town when they had some time off.

With the what, where and when thus roughly mapped out, it was time to figure out the how.

▲ (Above, left and right) The Berghof, 1944.

▼ Annotated plan of the Berghof.

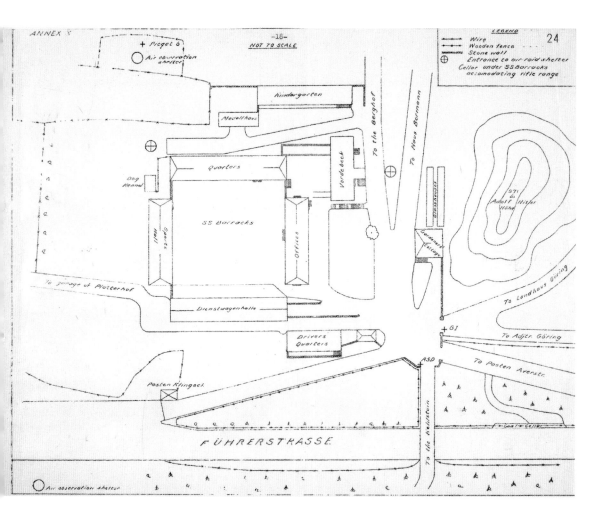

Map of the SS barracks at
the Berghof

The fine details

From the information gleaned from the captured guard, SOE knew that the best time to target Hitler would be while he walked alone and unprotected to the Teehaus on the Mooslahnerkopf Hill from the Berghof residence. Although not physically accompanied, the Führer would be kept under close observation by the SS patrol that followed him at a discreet distance, as well as by SS guards at the Gutshof for about 100 yards of the walk. He would also be visible to the SS guards at the Theaterhalle and the Landhaus Göring as he crossed the concrete by-pass from the Oberau road to the Führerstrasse. However, at this point, these guards would be more than 500 yards away.

Action at the Mooslahner Hill was nevertheless worthy of consideration in view of the fact that whereas a considerable interval of time may elapse between Hitler's visits to Schloss Klessheim and other FHQs, Hitler rarely missed his daily walk to the teahouse on the Mooslahner Hill. What's more, even if the sniper failed and Hitler reached the teahouse unharmed, it might be possible to bring a back-up plan into play, using the sniper's attempt as a diversion and attacking Hitler in his car on the return journey to the Berghof.

This secondary attempt would, in theory, be made by two agents firing a PIAT anti-tank gun or a bazooka from the woods in the vicinity of the Teehaus. These agents would not take up position until the arrival of the guard at the Teehaus after he had observed the sniper's failure to bring down Hitler. They would thus avoid the risk of detection by any guards or patrols in the neighbourhood of the Mooslahner Hill, because their attention would be drawn in the opposite direction. The guard, one may reasonably assume, would be sent for immediately following the first botched attempt and it's likely that they wouldn't suspect that another attack would be made.

Preparations

The scheme called for a sniper and a translator to be dropped into Austria by parachute. Having submitted their plan, SOE next recruited a German-speaking Pole and a British sniper for the operation, as well as a local shopkeeper from nearby Salzburg who had a detailed knowledge of the area and was known to be firmly anti-Nazi. Code named Heidentaler, the plan was that he would shelter the agents and transport them to Berchtesgaden disguised as German mountain troops – a disguise they would maintain as they moved on to the vantage point.

The sniper was duly briefed, and practised by firing at moving targets with a recalibrated Kar 98k fitted with a Mauser telescopic sight (the standard German Army sniper rifle) over ranges similar to those that would need to be covered at Berchtesgaden. The sniper would also be equipped with a 9mm Luger pistol fitted with a suppressor, which could be used to deal quickly and quietly with any Germans the sniper encountered while on the way to the firing position.

The plan is aborted

Although there was now a viable assassination plan and agents lined up to carry it out, there still remained the issue that some senior figures were opposed to it, particularly the deputy head of SOE's German Directorate, Lt Col Ronald Thornley. However, his superior, Sir Gerald Templer, and British Prime Minister Winston Churchill supported it.

What really scuppered the scheme, which was submitted in November 1944, was the controversy over whether it was actually worth killing Hitler at this point in war; by now, he was considered such a poor strategist that he was actually a liability for the Germans. It was felt that if he were replaced, whoever stepped in would probably do a better job of fighting the Allies and that this would prolong the war – an eventuality that was definitely not the intended outcome.

Thornley also argued that such an act was unnecessary, since Germany was already almost defeated. Furthermore, if Hitler were assassinated, he would likely become a martyr figure, and his death would cause people to wonder whether Germany might have won had Hitler survived. Given that the Allies wanted not only to defeat Nazism militarily but also to destroy it politically, anything that created a myth like this was to be avoided.

This lack of consensus and clash of views among senior members of SOE, coupled with the absence of further clear and reliable intelligence about Hitler's daily routine, ultimately meant that the plan was never put into action. The fact was simply that SOE had run out of time. Furthermore, it would not have worked, since Hitler left the Berghof for the last time on 14 July 1944, and never returned.

OPERATION *LONGSHANKS*
An operation against a German ship in Goa, India, 1943

Operation *Longshanks*, which was otherwise known as Operations *Boarding Party* and *Creek*, was a peculiar British operation undertaken on 9 March 1943 against a German merchant ship moored in the neutral Portuguese enclave of Goa in western India that had been covertly transmitting information to U-boats from Mormugao harbour. The mission remained secret until 1978 due to the fact that it was a serious infringement of Portuguese neutrality that could have political ramifications, but, once the story got out, the tale was told both in the 1978 book *Boarding Party* by James Leasor, and its later film adaptation, *The Sea Wolves* (1980).

The three German ships, *achenfels*, *Ehrenfels* and *aunfels*.

The Axis ships' movements

The ships had arrived in Mormugao harbour in two waves over the preceding four years before the operation was launched. The first to arrive, *Ehrenfels*, had departed Bhavnagar for Bombay on 28 August 1939, just three days before the war started, but instead slipped into Mormugao. On the following day, another German ship, *Drachenfels*, which had just left Goa for Rotterdam, returned to Mormugao. Three days later *Braunfels*, headed for Calcutta, also docked at Goa. One year later, in June 1940, the Italian ship *Anfora* also arrived.

The problem

At this time, a Bengali sympathetic to Germany provided information – such as the course, speed, destination and cargo of British ships departing Indian ports – to Robert Koch (code name 'Trompetta') the head of the German intelligence operation in Goa. This was then radioed by the *Ehrenfel*'s ship's radio officer, a code expert who by means of coded signals sent from a secret radio transmitter on board ship relayed the information to the captain of U-boat *181* – the leader of a U-boat pack that would then sink the Allied ships.

Given the neutral status of the enclave, there seemed no way for the British to deal with this matter by force; any open violation of neutrality could lead to either retaliation, a worsening of relations generally with other neutral countries, or, in the extreme, the entry of Portugal into the war on the Axis side. However, one thing was clear: the radio transmissions to the waiting U-boats had to be stopped. SOE was tasked with the job, commanded by Col Lewis Pugh of the Indian Police, who was also an SOE operative (and an honorary member of the Calcutta Light Horse).

Early attempts

SOE had already established its Indian mission, to become known as Force 136, in Meerut. The aims of the mission, set up by a former businessman, Colin Mackenzie of the J. and P. Coats clothing company, were to inspire and incite, organize, arm and equip indigenous national or ethnic resistance movements in Japanese-occupied territories. It was thus in Meerut that the SOE meeting, overseen by Mackenzie and Pugh, generated a plot to kidnap Robert Koch and his wife Grethe, and then bribe the captain of the *Ehrenfels* to take his ship to sea for seizure by the British.

Stewart and Pugh duly travelled to Goa in the guise of representatives of a trading company, and kidnapped Koch and his wife in December 1942, abducting them to India. Despite this, however, the German transmissions continued. It was obvious that another means had to be sought, so it was decided that Pugh and Stewart must meet with Roeffer, the captain of the

Ehrenfels, and offer him a payment of £20,000 to desert. This scheme didn't work either, however, so SOE decided it would have to act alone.

In light of all the activity and the abduction of Koch and his wife, the German Capt Roeffer ordered that explosive charges be fitted to the German vessels and trained the crews in a series of emergency procedures for opening the ships' seacocks and scuttling the vessels. When the Portuguese authorities heard about this, they ordered the explosive charges be removed, which they were, briefly; after the attempt to bribe him, Roeffer realized something was more immediately afoot and ordered that the charges be replaced.

The means to an end

The next solution came in the form of a group of civilians in reserved jobs as bankers, merchants and solicitors who were the remains of an old territorial unit called The Calcutta Light Horse, 1,400 miles away in Calcutta. The Calcutta Light Horse was a reserve unit of the Indian Army and had been inactive since the Boer War (1899–1902). Although in both the book and the film they were portrayed as being too old to be called up, in reality none of them was older than 33. Part of the problem now was convincing this group to take part in the raid by providing training and adequate transport for the voyage around the southern tip of India.

Of the reserve unit, 18 men were chosen for Operation *Longshanks*, four of whom came from the Calcutta Scottish Regiment. From these, Pugh was given the job of getting hold of the weaponry needed and with providing suitable training. The men were given no details about the operation and there was neither official backing nor funding. Each of the men simply took leave from his job, stating he was about to attend a training course near Goa, and started preparing for the mission. What's more, because the mission was supposedly unofficial, the men received no official recognition of their part in the war effort – not even the most basic war medals.

The operation

By 1942, the physical state of all four Axis merchant vessels was very poor, and many crew members had deserted, some of them seeking asylum in Goa, while others complained to the International Red Cross that they were being 'interned' by the Goan authorities.

Aware of the possibility that the unusual activity of taking a small craft out of service might be observed and the information passed on to the Germans, Pugh had to be very careful when finding a vessel for the long passage round India from Calcutta to Goa. He managed, however, obtaining a hopper barge called *Little Phoebe* and her Bengali crew. Such vessels were to be found in ports around the world, their task being to keep channels around ports clear by taking silt removed by a dredger out to sea, where it would be dumped. Given their purpose, these were inshore vessels intended for working in daylight and fair-weather conditions, not sailing round India.

Constructed as part of a pair in 1912, *Phoebe* was powered by a twin-screw propeller and possessed a maximum speed of less than 9 knots. It had a displacement of 1,200 tons with a length of 200ft, a beam of 38ft and a draught of 16ft. The barge made the passage via Trincomalee in Ceylon to Cochin, where it collected the men of the assault team, who had travelled across India by train via Madras, and then had to wait for four days for the barge to arrive. The barge then moved north-west along the coast of western India to Bombay as the attack party finalized its plan and divided into three teams: after boarding *Ehrenfels*, one party was to seize the bridge, the second to destroy the radio and the third to break the anchor chain.

Col E.H. Grice, who led the boarding party on *Ehrenfels*. ▶

A hopper barge, similar to the used in the mission. ▼

Two men did not embark on the barge at Cochin, but instead travelled overland to Goa with the task of decoying as many as possible of the German crew members away from the ship on the night scheduled for the attack. This they planned to achieve by paying the owner of a Goan brothel to offer free services that night to the seamen, and bribing a Goan official to host a party to which port officials and ships' officers would be invited. It was also arranged that there would be no taxis available to take the officers back to their ships.

On the night of 9/10 March, the boarding party headed by Col E.H. Grice met little opposition, and *Ehrenfel*'s radio equipment was quickly disabled, while the ship's captain and four of his men were killed in the fighting that followed. At this point, Roeffer's plan to demolish and scuttle the vessels was put into action. As previously described, he had anticipated the British move and had explosive charges fitted in each of the vessels so that in the event of an attack the ships would be scuttled rather than fall into British hands. As the British boarding party seized control of *Ehrenfels*, therefore, the charges were detonated and the ship sank.

According to witnesses, *Drachenfels* and *Braunfels* also burst into flames almost immediately after the *Ehrenfels* sounded the alarm, but the Italian *Anfora* only began burning about an hour later. Those on shore soon decided that the crews – nervous, depressed, fearful of a British attack and possibly drunk – had set fire to their own ships.

The barge, meanwhile, inconspicuously slipped out of the harbour, concerned that the Germans might have transmitted a final signal alerting the U-boats, one of which might possibly now search for *Little Phoebe*. This threat never materialized, however, and *Little Phoebe* wasn't attacked on its way back to Calcutta via Trincomalee. By the morning of the 9th, all four Axis vessels were on the floor of the harbour but continued burning for several days. The 100 or so surviving Axis personnel were rounded up by the Portuguese and put into an internment camp.

Effectiveness and recognition

In the forward to *Boarding Party*, the Earl Mountbatten of Burma wrote:

> This book tells how fourteen of them, with four colleagues from the Calcutta
> Scottish, another Auxiliary Force unit, volunteered for a hazardous task which, for
> reasons the author makes plain, no-one else was able to undertake. This happened

shortly before my arrival in India in 1943, as Supreme Allied Commander, South East Asia, and immediately saw how valuable were the results of this secret operation. I am pleased that at last credit may be given to those who planned and carried it out.

The effect of the mission is borne out by the facts. During the first 11 days of March 1943, three German U-boats – *U-160*, *U-182* and *U-506* – accounted for the sinking of 12 British, American, Norwegian and Dutch ships, a total of roughly 80,000 tons. Of these, *U-160* alone sank ten. However, after the success of Operation *Longshanks*, without the radio messages from *Ehrenfels* to give precise details of speed, destination, cargo and other material factors, U-boat commanders now had to rely only on luck. During the rest of March, the 13 German U-boats operating in the Indian Ocean only sank one ship, the *Panamanian Nortun* of 3,663 tons. Throughout the following month of April, their total was only three.

The Axis ships *Ehrenfels*, *Drachenfels*, *Braunfels* and *Anfora* were either salvaged and sold for scrap or disintegrated in the water.

OPERATION *SOURCE*
The attempt to sink the mighty *Tirpitz*, 1942

Developed by Cdr Cromwell-Varley using intelligence gathered by the Norwegian resistance, and especially brothers Torbjørn and Einar Johansen, Operation *Source* was a series of attacks carried out on 20–22 September 1943 at Kaa Fjord in northern Norway by X-class midget submarines against the heavy German warships *Tirpitz*, *Scharnhorst* and *Lützow*.

Early attempts

Prior to the 1943 attacks, a number of other operations were planned with the aim of sinking or incapacitating the *Tirpitz,* including several bombing raids by Fleet Air Arm. Then came Operation *Frodesley* – an unrealized Royal Navy plan by Adm Sir Max Horton, commander of the submarine forces in British waters – which involved the use of a fishing boat to secretly carry a midget submarine into the coastal waters of German-occupied Norway in March 1942.

Although never realized, *Frodesley* paved the way for the Operation *Title* attack on the German battleship in October 1942. This idea was a simple one: to tow the two manned Chariot torpedoes using a newly completed fishing boat, *Arthur*, until they were close to the target, then to set them off. A Norwegian, Leif Larsen, who had earlier escaped from Norway to Britain, was put in charge.

On the morning of 26 October, *Arthur* sailed for Norway and on the evening of the next day sighted the mountains around the island of Smolen. So far, so good. However, during the afternoon of 28 October, as *Arthur* was approaching the entrance to the fjord, the engine stopped; it was three hours before the crew could get it going again. To make matters worse, the generator used to recharge the Chariots' batteries also broke down and had to be thrown overboard, and as a final straw, the towing lugs on both of the Chariots snapped and the torpedoes drifted away and were lost. The mission was aborted.

The significance of the target

The Bismarck class battleship *Tirpitz* was named after Alfred von Tirpitz (1849–1930), a German Grand Admiral and Secretary of State of the German Imperial Naval Office – the administrative branch of the German Imperial Navy from 1897 until 1916. Prior to this, Prussia and the other German states had never had a strong navy, even after the German Empire was formed in 1871. Tirpitz, however, changed all this, taking the fledgling Imperial Navy and from the 1890s turning it into a force that would be able to compete in battle with the Royal Navy.

In addition to being a symbol of the German naval might, however, the Grand Admiral's namesake was selected as a target due to the fact that the incredibly powerful and well-armed battleship posed a grave threat to Allied shipping in Norway, where it had been sent in 1942 to act as a deterrent against an Allied invasion. Furthermore, *Tirpitz* also made two sorties to attempt to intercept Allied convoys to the Soviet Union in 1942, and the ship's presence forced the Royal Navy to keep sufficient resources in the area to keep *Tirpitz* 'bottled up'.

6 and crew prior to the operation, September 1943. ▼

The mission

The mission's objective was to destroy the *Tirpitz*, the battleship *Scharnhorst* and the heavy cruiser *Lützow*, which was in the nearby Langfjord, although since the *Scharnhorst* was out for exercises on the date of the attack, it could not be targeted.

The attack was masterminded and directed from the shore station HMS *Varbel*, located in Port Bannatyne on the Isle of Bute. Prior to the war, *Varbel* – named after Cdrs Varley and Bell, who were the architects of the X-craft prototype – had been the luxury 88-bedroom Kyles Hydropathic Hotel, but it was later requisitioned by the Admiralty to serve as the headquarters of the 12th Submarine Flotilla of mini-submarines. All X-craft training and preparation for attacks, including that on *Tirpitz*, was directed and coordinated from here.

In all, six X-craft were used: *X5*, *X6* and *X7* being allocated to attack the battleship *Tirpitz* in Kafjord, while *X9* and *X10* were to attack the battleship

X-craft at sea prior to the operation, September 1943.

Scharnhorst, also in Kafjord, and *X8* was to attack the heavy cruiser *Lützow* in the nearby Langfjord.

The mini-subs

Each X-craft mini-submarine was 51ft long, 5.5ft in diameter and displaced 27 tons surfaced and 30 tons submerged. Propulsion was by a four-cylinder diesel engine converted from a type used in London buses, and a 30hp electric motor, giving a maximum surface speed of 6.5 knots, and a submerged speed of 5.5 knots.

The crew initially numbered three – commander, pilot and engineer – but a specialist diver was added, for whom an airlock, known as a wet and dry compartment, was provided. The engineer operated and maintained most of the machinery in the vessel.

The X-craft carried two explosive charges held on opposite sides of the hull, each composed of 2 tons of amatol – a high explosive made from a mixture of TNT and ammonium nitrate. These would be dropped on the seabed underneath the target vessels and be detonated by a timed fuse. In addition, the mini-subs were equipped with electromagnets to neutralize detection by anti-submarine detection sensors.

The attack

The X-craft were towed to the area by conventional submarines – HMS *Truculent* (X6), *Syrtis* (X9), *Sea Nymph* (X8), *Thrasher* (X5), *Stubborn* (X7) and *Sceptre* (X10) – and manned by passage crews while underway. Once they were close to the targets, the operation crews would take over. Sadly, however, *X9* was lost with all hands during the passage when its towline broke and it sank abruptly because she had been rigged with a bow-down trim. *X8*, meanwhile, developed leaks in the side-mounted demolition charges, which had to be jettisoned and exploded, leaving no option but to scuttle the boat.

It is not quite clear what happened to *X5*, commanded by Lt Henty Henty-Creer, which disappeared with her crew during the course of Operation *Source*, but it is believed that the sub was sunk by a direct hit from one of *Tirpitz*'s 4in guns before the crew had a chance to place her charges.

X6 and *X7*, however, did make it, and managed to slip under the *Tirpitz*'s torpedo nets and each lay two mines on timer fuses below and around the

▲ HMS *Syrtis* and *X9* leaving port, 11 September 1943.

◀ HMS *Thrasher* and *X5* leaving port, 11 September 1943.

battleship on the seafloor. While trying to escape, both subs were detected and attacked. Of the eight crew members of the two craft, two were killed and the other six were captured by the Germans, survived the war, and were highly decorated for their actions. Both X-craft were abandoned.

This left just one sub, *X10*, which was originally intended to attack *Scharnhorst*. However, when it was discovered that *Scharnhorst* was engaged in exercises at the time, and hence was not at her normal mooring, the attack was abandoned – something that was also due to mechanical and navigation problems as much as the change of location. The submarine duly returned to rendezvous with her 'tug' submarine and was taken back to Scotland.

The damage inflicted

Despite the fact that only two of the six submarines reached their target, the mission was successful in that the charges those two subs laid inflicted very significant damage to key parts of *Tirpitz*, although not enough to sink it.

In terms of structural damage, shell plating was ripped open, the bottom of the ship was deformed by a large indentation, the wall of one of the fuel oil tanks was cracked, and bulkheads buckled in the double bottom, where more than 1,400 tons of water flooded into the fuel tanks and void space of the port

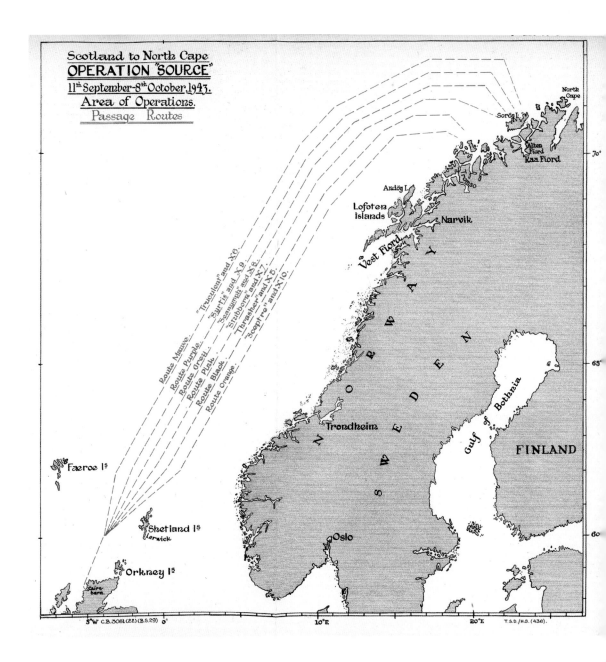

Scotland to North Cape
OPERATION "SOURCE"
11ᵗʰ September–8ᵗʰ October,1943.
Area of Operations.
Passage Routes

Route Mauve — "Truculent" and X6.
Route Purple — "Syrtis" and X9.
Route Green — "Seanymph" and X8.
Route Pink — "Stubborn" and X7.
Route Black — "Thrasher" and X5.
Route Orange — "Sceptre" and X10.

North Cape
Sorög I.
Alten Fiord
Kaa Fiord
Tromsö
Andög I.
Lofoten Islands
Narvik
Vest Fiord
N O R W A Y
S W E D E N
Gulf of Bothnia
FINLAND
Trondheim
Faeroe Iˢ
Shetland Iˢ
Lerwick
Oslo
Orkney Iˢ
Cairn barn

5°W C.B.3081(22)(B.S.29) 0°   10°E   20°E T.S.D./H.S.(436).

70°
65°
60°

▲ Plan of the passage routes for each of the X-craft.

side, causing the ship to list 1–2 degrees – something that could be redressed by the counter flooding of the port side. Above deck, Turret Dora was wrenched from its bearings – damage that was particularly problematic during the repair works since there wasn't a heavy crane in Norway that was capable of lifting the turret and replacing it in its correct alignment on its bearings.

In addition to all of this, water from the flooding played havoc with the turbo-generators, rendering all but one disabled. This was a highly engineered, integrated vessel full of sophisticated mechanical, electrical and electronic equipment, which meant that such damage severely hampered the ship's performance as a fighting vessel and put it out of action for six months while it was restored to full fitness by the repair ship *Neumark* in what has been described as one of the greatest and most complex feats of naval engineering of World War II. It thus wasn't until April 1944 that full speed trials could be carried out at Altafjord and the ship returned to active service.

The aftermath

For their part in putting the *Tirpitz* out of action for six months, the commanders of the X-craft, Lt Donald Cameron (*X6*) and Lt Basil Place (*X7*), were awarded the Victoria Cross, while Robert Aitken, Richard Haddon Kendall and John Thornton Lorimer received the Distinguished Service Order, and Edmund Goddard the Conspicuous Gallantry Medal. The commander of *X8*, John Elliott Smart, was appointed a Member of the Order of the British Empire (MBE).

Once the *Tirpitz* had returned to the water, the Royal Navy and Fleet Air Arm tried several times to sink it, and indeed managed to cause significant damage to the vessel and kill or wound hundreds of the crew – at a cost of several aircraft. The job of sinking the *Tirpitz* finally fell to the Royal Air Force during Operation *Catechism* (see page 170), which undertook no fewer than 13 bombing missions against the ship. Only four of these caused any significant damage, with the last one, involving 32 Lancaster bombers, finally sending the *Tirpitz* to the bottom of the ocean.

THE SINKING OF THE *BISMARCK*
The hunt to track down the pride of the Germany Navy

Introduction

At the start of World War II, the Royal Navy was the largest navy in the world. Key to its strength were its battlecruisers, such as HMS *Hood*. For over twenty years after this 46,680-ton behemoth was laid down in 1916 it remained the largest and most powerful warship in the world. In fact, Germany's Kreigsmarine lagged behind the Royal Navy at the outbreak of war in 1939, both in size and in capital ships, although it could undoubtedly claim an advantage in submarine warfare as the conflict progressed. Although there was a pre-war plan code named Plan Z to challenge the surface fleet of the Royal Navy through construction of aircraft carriers and battleships, resources were instead switched to U-boat production in 1939. Nevertheless, in 1936 *Bismarck* had already been laid down at Hamburg (along with Tirpitz, her sister ship, at Wilhelmshaven in the same year) and in 1940 she was commissioned into the Kriegsmarine. The worst fears of the British Admiralty had been realized, as this was a powerful warship capable of challenging any Royal Navy vessel on the high seas and it was believed that Germany was pushing for naval parity with Britain. As it was, the fate of *Hood* and *Bismarck* would become inextricably linked.

The Battle of the Denmark Straits

On 18 May 1941, the heavy cruiser *Prinz Eugen* slipped out into the Atlantic, with *Bismarck* following from Gotenhafen at 02:00 on 19 May – their mission, Operation *Rheinubung* (Rhine), being to attack Allied shipping. This was the kind of moment that *Hood* had been designed for all those years ago. Swedish sources were able to bring word to the Admiralty that the two German ships had broken out into the Atlantic, and *Hood* and HMS *Prince of Wales* set off in hot pursuit. The resources devoted by the Admiralty to

Aerial photograph of the
›sition of the Bismarck in
ay 1941.

hunting down *Bismarck* was a sign of how seriously she was taken. Six battleships; three battlecruisers; 16 cruisers; two aircraft carriers; 33 destroyers; and eight submarines would eventually be engaged in this operation. Meanwhile, HMS *Suffolk* and HMS *Norfolk* were plotting the movements of *Bismarck* and *Prinz Eugen*, reporting their locations via radar. On 24 May 1941, *Hood* and *Prince of Wales* first came into contact with *Bismarck* and *Prinz Eugen* and both ships opened fire from a range of

TO I D 8 G   ZTP/1054

FROM GERMAN NAVAL SECTION G C AND C S

110/4595 KC/S   TO: 0025/27/5/41

                TOO 0153

TO FLEET W 70

ENEMY REPORT:

TO C IN C AFLOAT:

I THANK YOU IN THE NAME OF THE ENTIRE GERMAN PEOPLE. ADOLF

HITLER

TO THE CREW OF THE BATTLESHIP BISMARCK:

ALL GERMANY IS WITH YOU. ALL THAT CAN STILL BE DONE, WILL BE

DONE. YOUR DEVOTION TO DUTY WILL FORTIFY OUR PEOPLE IN THEIR

STRUGGLE FOR EXISTENCE. ADOLF HITLER.

TOO 2229/29/5/41+++AGT+++

◀ Decrypted message from Hitler on 27 May, congratulating *Bismarck*'s crew.

Log of deaths on HMS *Prince of Wales* caused by the action against *Bismarck* on 24 May 1941. ▼

1218 %c 255°. 1224 %c 250°. 1226 %c 240°. 29 Knots.

1231. Altered to port to 350°. 1233. 27 Kn. 1236. %c 235°.

1237. 26 Knots. 1240 %c 250°. 27 Kn. 1244 %c 240°.

Course approx 240° as required to follow 'Bismarck'. and 'Prinz Eugen'.

Currents experienced			RETURN OF DEATHS		ANCHOR BEARINGS		
DATE OF DEATH	NAME OF DECEASED	SEX	AGE	RANK OR OCCUPATION	LAST PLACE OF ABODE	CAUSE OF DEATH	NATIONALITY
May. 24. 1941	Norman Johnstone	Male	17 years	Boy Sig. D/JX 162832	H.M.S 'Prince of Wales'	Enemy Action	Scottish.
May. 24. 1941	Edward James Hunt	Male	22 years	Act. Ldg. Sig. D/JX 141718	H.M.S 'Prince of Wales'	Enemy Action.	English.
May. 24. 1941	Walter Graham Andrews	Male	20 years	Act. ldg. Sig D/JX 147668	H.M.S 'Prince of Wales'	Enemy Action	Welsh.
May. 24. 1941	Mervyn Richard Tucker	Male	21 years	Ldg. Sea. D/JX 143147	H.M.S 'Prince of Wales'	Enemy Action	English.
May. 24. 1941	Thornton Smith	Male	21 years	Ord. Sea. D/JX 197804	H.M.S 'Prince of Wales'	Enemy Action	English
May. 24. 1941	Thomas Ronald Slater	Male	20 years	Able Sea. D/JX 152140	H.M.S 'Prince of Wales'	Enemy Action	English
May. 24. 1941	Leslie Maddocks Deeds	Male	21 years	Able Sea. D/SSX 28435	H.M.S 'Prince of Wales'	Enemy Action	English
May. 24. 1941	Harry Hallam	Male	33 years	Able Sea. D/JT 112521	H.M.S 'Prince of Wales'	Enemy Action	English
May. 24. 1941	Arthur Molyneux Harper	Male	28 years	Able Sea R/af P/JX 190694	H.M.S 'Prince of Wales'	Enemy Action	English
May. 24. 1941	Edward Brian Diamond	Male	21 years	Ord. Sea D/JX 206256	H.M.S 'Prince of Wales'	Enemy Action	English.
May 24 1941	Dreyer		17 years	Midshipman R.N.	H.M.S 'Prince of Wales'	Enemy Action	English
May 24 1941	John Brat Ince	Male	18 years	Midshipman R.N.	H.M.S 'Prince of Wales'	Enemy Action	English
May 24. 1941	Fairbairn	Male	—	Ord. Sea R.D/F	H.M.S 'Prince of Wales'	Enemy Action	—
May 24. 1941	Barlow	Male	—	Ord. Sea R.D/F	H.M.S 'Prince of Wales'	Enemy Action	—

Number on Sick List   16

1325 %c 140°. 1340 %c 180°. 1410 %c 200°. 1437 %c 190°.

1440 %c 180°. 1445 %c 160°. 1455 %c 170°. 1504 %c 180°.

1518 Sighted 1 Catalina bearing 210°.

1531 Suffolk bore 255°. 6¾'.

1630. Zig-Zag No. 10.

1715 'Prince of Wales' astern. Co 180°. 24 Knots. Resume zig-zag.

25,000 yards. It was during this engagement that a fire started amidships on board *Hood*; shortly after, a shell fired from *Bismarck* penetrated the lightly armoured deck causing a catastrophic explosion that tore the ship apart. *Hood* sank in just three minutes; there were only three survivors from a crew of 1,419 men. Meanwhile, Capt Leach of *Prince of Wales* broke off the engagement and escaped under smoke cover at 06:13 after the ship suffered a number of hits. *Hood*'s loss profoundly shocked the Admiralty, which assembled every available warship in the vicinity to hunt *Bismarck* down. A Sunderland patrol aircraft which arrived on the scene reported that *Bismarck* had been damaged in the exchange and was trailing oil. The stage was set for a showdown between the Royal Navy and its German nemesis.

The pursuit

Following the news of the battle, Adm Somerville, commander of Force H, consisting of the battleship *Renown*, the aircraft carrier *Ark Royal* and the cruiser *Sheffield*, was ordered north. At the same time, Adm Tovey was ordered to intercept *Bismarck* using the aircraft carrier *Victorious* and her escorts. Taking up a position 100 miles from the German force, nine Fairey Swordfish aircraft of 825 Naval Air Squadron were despatched at 22:00 and in poor weather conditions they located the *Bismarck* and launched their torpedoes. The ninth of these actually struck its target amidships, resulting in damage to collision mats and the flooding of one of the boiler rooms through a shell hole, as the ship manoeuvred to avoid the torpedo. Although *Bismarck* was able to reduce speed somewhat, and new collision mats were prepared to stem further flooding, the loss of boilers and new maximum speed of 28 knots posed a dilemma for Adm Lütjens. Clearly the original mission he had set out on could not now be fulfilled with the ship so badly compromised. The nearest safe ports were Bergen or Trondheim but they were a thousand miles across hazardous seas, while the alternative option was to dock at St-Nazaire in occupied France. He chose the latter. Having been shadowed at various stages by *Suffolk*, *Norfolk* and *Prince of Wales*, *Bismarck* escaped and made for the coast of France.

The search

Adm Tovey had divided his vessels to cover escape routes and, under the assumption that *Bismarck* was now headed for France, he signalled Adm Somerville of Force H to ensure that positions were taken up.

IMPORTANT   NOTWT
ANY REPLY TO THIS MESSAGE
IR TO BE ENDORSED NOTWT

27 MAY 1941

C.G.P.
NWD   NR 111   IMPORTANT   NOT W/T
PASS TO SELF   GRS NIL

ADDRESSED TO:-   15 = 16 = 18 = 19 GROUPS = PRU BENSON
FROM:-   H.Q.C.C.
OPS 582   27/5
ENSURE THAT ALL WHO TOOK PART IN RECENT OPERATION HAVE FOLLOWING
MESSAGE AND REPLY BROUGHT TO THEIR NOTICE. TO A O C IN C COASTAL
COMMAND FROM ADMIRALTY. ADMIRALTY WISH GRATEFULLY TO ACKNOWLEDGE
THE PART PLAYED BY THERECONNAISANCE OF THE FORCE UNDER YOUR COMMAND
WHICH CONTRIBUTED IN A LARGE MEASURE TO THE SUCCESSFUL OUTCOME OF
THE RECENT OPERATIONS . TO ADMIRALTY FROM A O C IN C COASTAL
COMMAND . YOUR MESSAGE VERY MUCH APPRECIATED AND HAS BEEN
REPEATED TO ALL CONCERNED. IT WAS A GREAT HUNT AND WE ARE ALL
EAGER AND READY FOR MORE   ====   2130
QQ
BRADBURY   BB/KKKK

NWD   R   2245   COOPER   BBBBB

An intercepted message from *Bismarck* was plotted incorrectly, however, resulting in Adm Tovey's ships sailing further from the escaping battleship in the belief that she was sailing for harbour in Germany through the Iceland-Faroes gap. Later that afternoon, the error was corrected with a signal indicating to Tovey that *Bismarck* was heading for France, and throughout 25 May the Catalina flying boats of Coastal Command were out searching. Thus, once again, the Royal Navy was converging on *Bismarck* after a period when her whereabouts were unknown.

▲ Messages from the Admiralty to the AOC and in response showing appreciatic for the role of the AOC in the hunt for *Bismarck*.

The battle

At 10:30 on 26 May, a flying boat from 209 Squadron spotted *Bismarck*. It transmitted a wireless message to say that the battleship was 700 miles north-west of Brest in France. Adm Tovey was still 130 miles away – having closed the gap somewhat overnight – and *Rodney* had joined *Repulse*, *Prince of Wales*, *Victorious* and *Norfolk* in pursuit. Force H was in the best position, only 70 miles to the east. The best option seemed to be to attempt to slow *Bismarck* down by launching a Swordfish attack. At 14:50 fourteen Swordfish took off from *Ark Royal*, under Somerville's command. A number of ships, including *Victorious*, *Prince of Wales*, *Suffolk* and *Repulse* were short of fuel at this point and so had to break off the chase; only *King George V* and *Rodney* had any chance of reaching their target. Nevertheless, a close shave ensued as the Swordfish mistook *Sheffield* for *Bismarck* in poor weather; thankfully all of the torpedoes failed to hit or detonated on impact with the sea. A second attack was hastily arranged, with the torpedo fuses replaced for greater reliability. This time, 15 Swordfish took off and, taking their final directions from *Sheffield*, made their attack at 20:47. Under intense anti-aircraft fire, two torpedoes managed to hit their target – one amidships and the other exploding right aft. This left *Bismarck* effectively crippled, mainly because her rudder was now out of action, although there was also further structural damage with some flooding.

During that night, Capt Vian's 4th Destroyer Flotilla shadowed *Bismarck*. His aim was twofold: to deliver the battleship into the hands of the Royal Navy, or to sink or stop her with torpedoes during the night. This was easier

etailed 3D drawing of the
ttleship HMS *Rodney*
owing how she was fitted out
prioritize her firepower. ▼

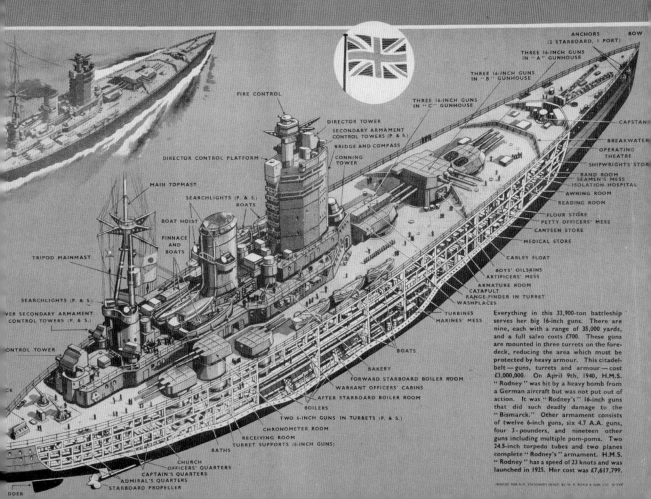

VERY ACTIVE SERVICE – THE BRITISH BATTLESHIP H.M.S. "RODNEY"

ANCHORS (2 STARBOARD, 1 PORT)
BOW
THREE 16-INCH GUNS IN "A" GUNHOUSE
THREE 16-INCH GUNS IN "B" GUNHOUSE
THREE 16-INCH GUNS IN "C" GUNHOUSE
FIRE CONTROL
DIRECTOR TOWER
SECONDARY ARMAMENT CONTROL TOWERS (P. & S.)
BRIDGE AND COMPASS
CONNING TOWER
DIRECTOR CONTROL PLATFORM
CAPSTANS
BREAKWATER
OPERATING THEATRE
SHIPWRIGHTS' STOR
BAND ROOM
SEAMEN'S MESS
ISOLATION HOSPITAL
AWNING ROOM
READING ROOM
MAIN TOPMAST
SEARCHLIGHTS (P. & S.)
BOATS
BOAT HOIST
FLOUR STORE
PETTY OFFICERS' MESS
CANTEEN STORE
MEDICAL STORE
PINNACE AND BOATS
TRIPOD MAINMAST
CARLEY FLOAT
BOYS' OILSKINS
ARTIFICERS' MESS
ARMATURE ROOM
CATAPULT
RANGE-FINDER IN TURRET
WASHPLACES
SEARCHLIGHTS (P. & S.)
VER SECONDARY ARMAMENT CONTROL TOWERS (P. & S.)
ONTROL TOWER
TURBINES
MARINES' MESS
BOATS
BAKERY
FORWARD STARBOARD BOILER ROOM
WARRANT OFFICERS' CABINS
AFTER STARBOARD BOILER ROOM
BOILERS
TWO 6-INCH GUNS IN TURRETS (P. & S.)
CHRONOMETER ROOM
RECEIVING ROOM
TURRET SUPPORTS (6-INCH GUNS)
BATHS
CHURCH
OFFICERS' QUARTERS
CAPTAIN'S QUARTERS
ADMIRAL'S QUARTERS
STARBOARD PROPELLER
DDER

Everything in this 33,900-ton battleship serves her big 16-inch guns. There are nine, each with a range of 35,000 yards, and a full salvo costs £700. These guns are mounted in three turrets on the fore-deck, reducing the area which must be protected by heavy armour. This citadel-belt — guns, turrets and armour — cost £3,000,000. On April 9th, 1940, H.M.S. "Rodney" was hit by a heavy bomb from a German aircraft but was not put out of action. It was "Rodney's" 16-inch guns that did such deadly damage to the "Bismarck." Other armament consists of twelve 6-inch guns, six 4.7 A.A. guns, four 3-pounders, and nineteen other guns including multiple pom-poms. Two 24.5-inch torpedo tubes and two planes complete "Rodney's" armament. H.M.S. "Rodney" has a speed of 23 knots and was launched in 1925. Her cost was £7,617,799.

PRINTED FOR H.M. STATIONERY OFFICE BY W. R. ROYLE & SON, LTD. 5/2397

said than done. A destroyer had to be located astern and on the bow and quarter of *Bismarck*, and all in fading light. Exchanges between the destroyers and *Bismarck* ensued, as *Piorun*, manned by Commander Plawski and other Polish crew members, opened fire. In the process, *Piorun* became detached

Map showing the chase and sinking of the *Bismarck*, 23–27 May 1941. ▼

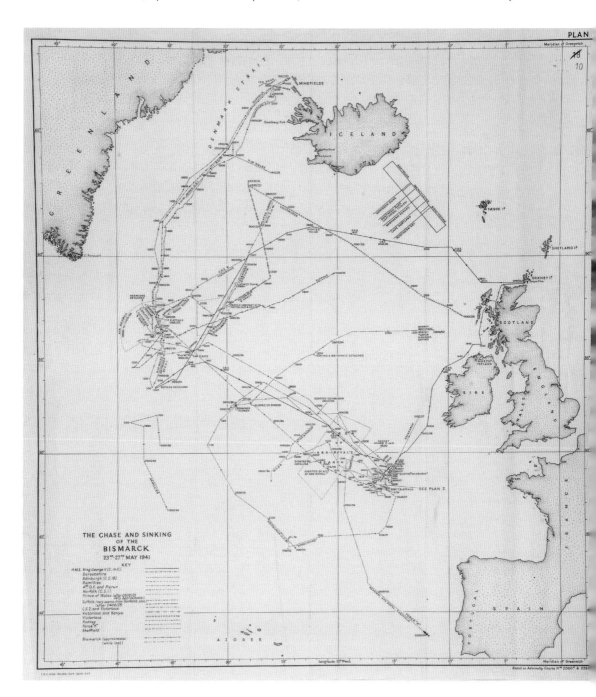

from the main destroyer force. The remaining destroyers under Vian's command – *Maori*, *Cossack* and *Zulu* – set up a torpedo attack later that evening, but these torpedoes missed their target. The conditions were too tricky for accurate firing, with a heavy swell and in complete darkness. By 04:00 the destroyers had lost contact with *Bismarck*.

Nevertheless, as daylight dawned on 27 May, *Bismarck* was in range of *King George V*, *Rodney* and *Norfolk*. Circling, because of her jammed rudder, *Bismarck* was a sitting target. *King George V* opened fire, followed by *Rodney*, while *Norfolk* also opened fire from a range of 10 miles. *Bismarck* returned fire, with some of her shells coming close to *Rodney*, but in truth it was the German battleship now registering numerous hits – increasingly so as *King George V* and *Rodney* manoeuvred their full broadsides towards their target. As this was happening, the *Devonshire* joined in from the south.

As *Bismarck* was increasingly engulfed in explosions, the rate of her return fire decreased significantly. This was probably hastened by one of *Rodney*'s shells, which at 09:02 struck her bridge area, almost certainly killing *Bismarck*'s bridge crew and Capt Lütjens in the process. Another wrecked the forward gun battery. This enabled the Royal Navy to close in further; *Rodney*

Map showing the route taken to approach the *Bismarck* and action against her on 27 May 1941. ▼

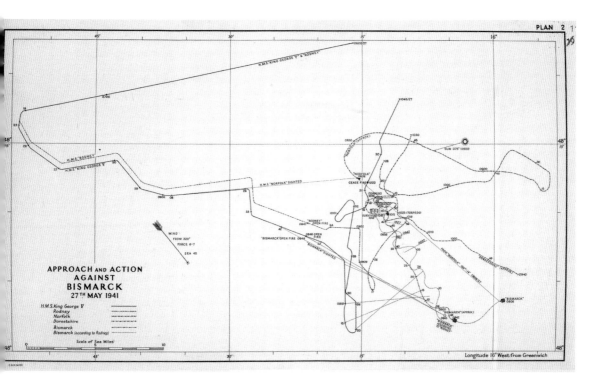

approached to 4 miles, firing her guns while continually reloading her torpedo tubes. In total, Tovey's ships fired several hundred shells in that short space of time, and over 2,800 were fired by the four ships in combination (400 of them scoring hits). By around 10:00 *Bismarck* was wrecked and in flames. The order was given by the first officer to abandon ship, and explosive charges were set to scuttle her; these duly detonated. Two torpedoes fired by *Dorsetshire* struck *Bismarck* below the waterline around this time, and she listed heavily. With hundreds of men now in the water, *Maori* and *Dorsetshire* moved in to pull them out with ropes. At 10:36 the *Bismarck* sank, with just 115 survivors out of a crew of over 2,200.

This was the end for Germany's greatest battleship, which had posed such a threat to Atlantic convoys. This action is considered a major turning point in the Battle of the Atlantic, neutralizing the threat from Germany's surface fleet and leaving the task of sinking Allied merchant shipping to U-boats.

OPERATION *MARKET GARDEN*
The raid that proved to be a bridge too far, 1944

The summer of 1944 had been a critical moment for the Western Allies. An extraordinary landing on the beaches of Normandy supported by a complicated airborne operation had seen them establish a solid foothold in Nazi-occupied France with a logistical link back across the English Channel. Though now considered the beginning of the end and ultimately successful in its goals, Operation *Overlord* had proved costly and at times had stretched the forces involved to their limits. What is more, victory on the beaches did not precipitate a collapse of the enemy, and the fighting that followed was hard and in certain areas stagnated.

For the forces under British command in the east of the lodgement this was especially true, with Caen proving to be a particularly hard nut to crack. Seen as the pivot around which FM Bernard Montgomery would shift his forces, it was eventually taken after lengthy fighting through June and July 1944, leading to more mobile warfare up to the Belgian-Dutch frontier. Pushing inland from their western beachhead, American forces had on the whole made swifter progress into the occupied French interior, pushing before them the retreating German Army, weakened by its commitments around Caen. With the Battle of France won, the combined Allied forces, under the ultimate

Gen Sir Bernard Montgomery.

direction of the Supreme Allied Commander, the American Gen Eisenhower, needed to decide on a route to Berlin.

▲ Winston Churchill, Gen Montgomery, Gen Guy Symonds and Gen Sir Miles Dempsey.

Next steps

Just how the advance into Germany would be taken forwards from this point was contentious. American and British thinking differed, with the latter believing a now shattered and retreating German Army could be pushed back through the Low Countries and a foothold could be established over the Rhine in Holland. From here, the Allies would be able to swing up through the Ruhr valley, thereby denying the Nazi war effort of its industrial heartland and bringing an end to hostilities that year. So convinced was he of this narrow thrust, Montgomery pushed Eisenhower hard to allow him the resources and command to deliver the final punch to knock the enemy out of the war. Eisenhower's own instinct and the arguments of his American subordinate commanders, however, led him to a compromise. What was eventually approved under Montgomery's command was a scaled-back operation to secure a bridgehead over the Lower Rhine; it was to be called Operation *Market Garden*.

Sketch showing details of the routes taken to Arnhem. ▶

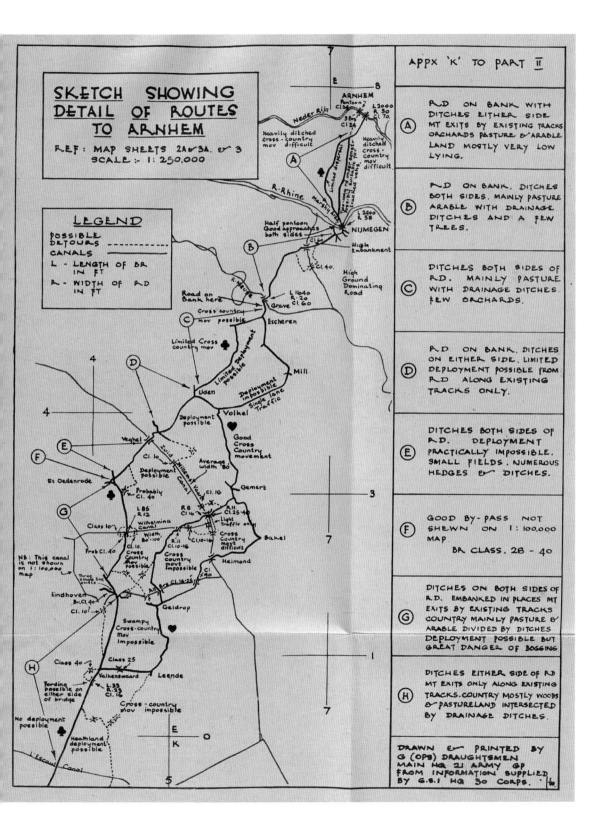

The plan

Market Garden was first and foremost an airborne operation. Used to some success on D-Day – particularly the glider-borne troops who secured the River Orne and Caen Canal crossings ahead of the landings – these forces had otherwise not yet played a decisive role in the conflict for either side, with even the German use on Crete proving costly and not delivering against expectations. Nonetheless, Montgomery's plan was to blanket with paratroops the hinterland either side of the 64-mile road between the Belgian-Dutch border and the Rhine road and rail bridges at Arnhem. Gen Brian Horrocks' British XXX Corps would push up the road through the by-then secured positions of the US 101st Airborne Division at Eindhoven and the US 82nd Airborne Division at Nijmegen, before reaching the Anglo-Polish I Airborne Corps at Arnhem. Montgomery believed it would take

Annotated map showing the position of the bridge and the hospital at Arnhem. ▼

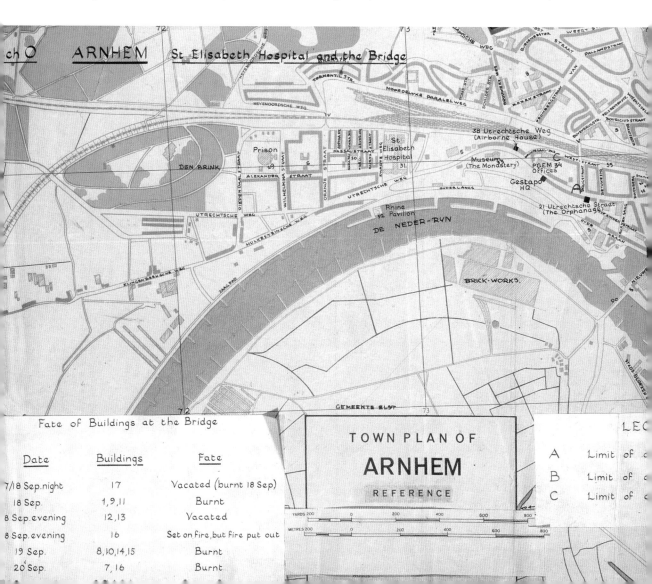

ch O ARNHEM St. Elisabeth Hospital and the Bridge

38 Utrechtsche Weg (Airborne House)

Prison

St. Elisabeth Hospital 31

Museum (The Monastery)

PGEM 34 Offices

DEN BRINK

Gestapo HQ

21 Utrechtsche Straat (The Orphanage)

Rhine Pavilion

DE NEDER-RYN

BRICK-WORKS.

GEMEENTE ELST

Fate of Buildings at the Bridge

Date	Buildings	Fate
7/18 Sep. night	17	Vacated (burnt 18 Sep)
18 Sep.	1,9,11	Burnt
18 Sep. evening	12,13	Vacated
18 Sep. evening	16	Set on fire, but fire put out
19 Sep.	8,10,14,15	Burnt
20 Sep.	7,16	Burnt

TOWN PLAN OF ARNHEM

REFERENCE

YARDS 200   0   200   400   600   800
METRES 200   0   200   400   600   800

LEG

A   Limit of c
B   Limit of c
C   Limit of c

two days for the main body to reinforce the airborne units on the Rhine; not everyone was so confident.

Lt Gen Frederick 'Boy' Browning, commanding British I Airborne Corps, is famed for having uttered the prosaic line 'we might be going a bridge too far', while his subordinate commanding the Polish Parachute Brigade, Gen Stanisław Sosabowski, believed the plans were not only underestimating German strength in the area but appeared ignorant of the significance of Arnhem to the Germans as a gateway into their country. The commander of British 2nd Army, Gen Sir Miles Dempsey, remained concerned about enemy strength, particularly intelligence suggesting that panzer forces mauled in the Battle of France were regrouping and refitting in Holland. The planning also ignored reports about enemy strength originating from the Dutch resistance, and neglected to call on their support. No doubt a reaction to the Nordpol Affair earlier in the war – where the Germans had managed to infiltrate and undo British intelligence efforts in the country – this decision denied British and Polish units a better understanding of what they were about to drop in to.

H-Hour and first encounters

On 17 September, the day the operation was launched, the German forces across the 75-mile front were understrength and weakly supported by armour and artillery. However, Gen Gustav-Adolf von Zangen's 15th Army was attempting to withdraw north-east from the Channel coast towards southern Holland, bringing up to another 100,000 men to join the German defences and to threaten the flanks of XXX Corps' advance. As Dutch intelligence reports had suggested, the remains of Gen Wilhelm Bittrich's efficient II SS Panzer Corps – the 9th SS and 10th SS Divisions – were also in the Arnhem-Nijmegen area resting and refitting.

153

By midday on 17 September 1944, the largest airborne armada ever to take flight for a single mission was in the air and moving towards Holland. The first three lifts were made up of 4,700 aircraft carrying more than 20,000 soldiers, 511 vehicles, 330 pieces of artillery and a further 590 tons of ammunition and equipment. Rather than throwing the surprised Germans into a panicked and dispersed defence, however, FM Gerd von Rundstedt – in overall command of German forces in the west – adeptly coordinated his forces after he quickly identified the object of the Allied offensive: the Arnhem and Nijmegen bridges.

▲ Paratroopers and gliders taking part in Operation *Market Garden*, during which the Allies dropped almost 9,000 paratroopers behind German lines. Only some 2,000 survived. (Corbis via Getty Images)

The bridge at Arnhem

The first reports of the landings began around 13:30 and the reaction was swift, with the most experienced German units rapidly making their way towards the sounds of gunfire. An airborne assault is at its most vulnerable during the landing stage, when forces are dispersed, something that was not lost on the German defenders. By the end of the first day they had organized defensive lines and dispatched aggressive patrols, which inflicted significant casualties on the British 1st Parachute Brigade when it attempted to break out of its landing zone. Nonetheless, as darkness was falling, the 2nd Battalion Parachute Regiment (2 Para) reached the bridge at Arnhem and established itself at the northern end.

It was in part these actions that led to the first of five Victoria Crosses that were issued during *Market Garden*. Lt John Grayburn of 2 Para had led an assault over the Arnhem bridge on the evening of 17 September that had been driven back, during which he was shot through the shoulder. He nonetheless organized the defences at the northern end and repulsed spirited German attacks the following morning and over the next three days, inflicting heavy casualties. He was eventually killed by a tank on 20 September.

Despite failing to push the British from the bridge, German forces had managed to prevent reinforcements from getting through to the isolated 2 Para. The most concerted effort to reach them took place on the morning of 19 September under the cover of mist but broke down into costly disorder as it cleared. Exposed to the full force of German defences on the opposite bank of the Rhine, the men of 1, 3 and 11 Para, and 2nd Battalion South Staffordshire Regiment, were cut down in droves. A further two Victoria Crosses were won on 19 September: one in the air where Flt Lt David Lord braved intense anti-aircraft fire to deliver supplies to the beleaguered airborne forces on the ground and ultimately paid with his life; and the other on the ground for Capt Lionel Queripel of the 10 Para, who was killed after reorganizing disparate forces under heavy fire and continuing to fight, and then covering the withdrawal of his men when there was no hope of further advance.

The remnants of 2 Para held out at the bridge until around 11:00 on 21 September when their ammunition was gone and the Germans opposite effectively demolished the houses in which they had established their defence. German forces could now cross the bridge in an attempt to head off the advance of XXX Corps.

1st Airborne Division bridgehead, Oosterbeek

The drop zones of the British and Polish airborne forces who entered the battle between 17 and 19 September were some distance from their primary objectives. Given the unexpected level of opposition and the speed with which the German Army responded, it is less surprising in hindsight that the bulk of the force failed to make the bridge at Arnhem. With half of their initial strength required to hold the landing grounds and after a dash for the bridge in vehicles in the early stages of the battle came to naught, there was little else the infantrymen could do in the face of stiffening German opposition.

After the final failed attempt to reach 2 Para on 19 September, the bulk of the force remained bottled up within a shrinking perimeter at Oosterbeek. With increasing quantities of German armour being committed to the fight – something they were underequipped to deal with – the defensive perimeter was hammered from the outside and fierce fighting ensued almost without respite. It was in this fighting that a further two Victoria Crosses were won, both largely in connection with the attempted destruction of German tanks and both to men of the same unit – the South Staffordshire Regiment. LSgt John Baskeyfield single-handedly manned a number of six-pounder anti-tank guns after his and other crews had been killed, keeping the guns in action until he was killed by fire from one of his targets. Maj Robert Cain – the only VC winner to survive the battle – was commended for his leadership in the defence of the Oosterbeek perimeter and determined use of the PIAT (a man-portable anti-tank weapon) against German armour.

Despite this resistance, German forces regained control of the landing zones, and the bulk of supplies dropped by the RAF for 1st Airborne Division were captured. Under increasing pressure, running out of ammunition, food and water, and suffering irreplaceable casualties, the remnants of Maj Gen Roy Urquhart's division managed to hold out until 25 September. Worn down and unable to fight offensively, and with their relief in the form of XXX Corps still south of the Rhine, they were forced to retire across the river during the night, abandoning the bridgehead.

The road to Nijmegen

The second part of the *Market Garden* operation – an armoured thrust through the German front line that would drive through to Nijmegen along roads secured on either side by further airborne drops – had also suffered setbacks. Although the drops of the US 101st and 82nd Airborne had gone well, the progress of XXX Corps was not as brisk as had been hoped, thanks in the most part to stiffer-than-expected defences and German attempts to sever the route of advance laterally. Waiting for the tanks of XXX Corps, the

Americans found themselves bogged down in defensive battles that restricted the 82nd's ability to push out into Nijmegen to secure the River Waal crossings, while the 101st were within a stone's throw of the bridge at Son when it was blown by the Germans. The delays this caused the advance allowed the 10th SS Panzer Division to establish itself in Nijmegen.

Having to erect its own crossing at Son cost XXX Corps more valuable time, as did fighting its way into Nijmegen without secure bridges across the Waal. The bridges eventually fell in a concerted effort on 20 September, with armoured elements of XXX Corps pushing into Nijmegen with the support of American paratroopers, and a daring but costly river crossing by the 3rd Battalion of the American 504th Parachute Infantry Regiment. In broad daylight and under intense machine gun and mortar fire, they used boats to cross the Waal in a successful effort to loop round and attack the northern end of the bridge. With their flank now vulnerable and tanks of the Grenadier Guards forcing their way across the bridge, the Germans withdrew.

eptember 1944: Allied
herman tanks crossing the
wly captured bridge at
megen. (Keystone/Getty
ages) ▼

It was around 19:00 by the time the crossing had been made and there seemed little possibility that the isolated force available would be able to push through the remaining 7 miles in darkness on unreconnoitred roads and against an unknown enemy. As it was, XXX Corps' narrow line of communications rearward back to the Belgian frontier – the road up which its supplies and reinforcements had to travel – was under constant pressure from artillery and infiltrations from scratch forces of infantry and tanks. The decision was made to halt and reinforce the bridgehead over the Waal before taking up the advance in support of 1st Airborne Division the following

Paratroopers search for German soldiers in the rubble of the streets. (Corbis via Getty Images) ▼

morning. Unbeknown to them, however, by this stage 2 Para's hold on the north end of the bridge at Arnhem was all but collapsing.

The vanguard of XXX Corps would not reach the Rhine until 24 September, too late for 2 Para. Despite linking up with Polish forces held up in Driel south of the river and providing artillery support to the beleaguered 1st Airborne Division on the north bank, the offensive had stalled. Gen Dempsey ordered the evacuation of Oosterbeek and the end of *Market Garden*.

Aftermath

Despite optimistic assessments from the likes of Montgomery, *Market Garden* had been a costly endeavour that had ultimately failed to achieve its objectives. Although XXX Corps had suffered in the region of 1,500 casualties and the Americans nearly 4,000, the gallant if ultimately futile stand of 1st Airborne Division (both British and Polish elements) had cost more than 7,500 men. Dutch civilians also suffered greatly in the crossfire and through Nazi reprisals in the battle's aftermath.

Blighted with problems from the outset, some of which were more predictable than others, in reality the whole plan of operations had suffered from a number of weaknesses. In the first instance, and probably most importantly, it took little account of the German Army's proven ability to rapidly

Crowds dancing in the streets following the liberation of Eindhoven. ▼

react and slow Allied advances. It also demanded that XXX Corps shrug off some of its inherent caution, reliance on artillery and desire for secure lines of communication – something drilled into the British Army since 1942. Finally, the entire operation pivoted on the ability of lightly armed airborne forces to hold ground and secure objectives ahead of the main attacking force. Though the British, Polish and American contingents had managed this in part and generally against the odds, the task in light of the opposition they faced was simply too great. Despite many examples of individual courage and some local if short-lived successes, *Market Garden* was in the end a failure. Montgomery had indeed set his sights on a bridge too far.

OPERATION *CHASTISE*

The Dambuster raid by Bomber Command's 617 Squadron, 1943

Operation *Chastise* was the famous 'Dambusters' raid by Bomber Command's newly formed 617 Squadron, which took place on the night of 16/17 May 1943. A specialized 'bouncing bomb', which was developed by Barnes Wallis, was used in the attack on four dams in the Ruhr district.

The concept for the raid was long in the making, as the Air Ministry had identified the heavily industrialized Ruhr as a major target even before World War II began. In particular, much of this industrial activity depended on four dams in the Ruhr district: the Möhne, the Sorpe, the Lister and the Ennepe. Two dams in the Weser district were also identified: the Eder and the Diemel.

The 'bouncing bomb'

Barnes Wallis' 'bouncing bomb' really made the mission possible. Without such an invention, the destruction of a dam would prove difficult as the damage had to take place at the base of the dam wall to have any chance of breaching it. His designs show how he intended the bomb to function.

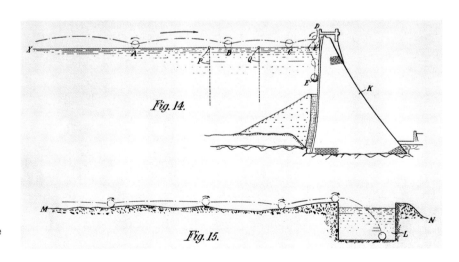

Fig. 14.

Fig. 15.

Barnes Wallis' plans for the 'bouncing bomb.' ▶

CRFN/AS

Telephone: Shrewsbury 4401.

Research Department,

Shrewsbury,

SALOP.

6A

2nd April, 1941.

S E C R E T.

Air Marshal Sir Richard E.C. Peirse, K.C.B.,D.S.O.,A.F.C.,R.A.F.,
  Bomber Command,
    C/o G.P.O.,
      High Wycombe

Dear Air Marshal,

I am very sorry not to have had the opportunity of seeing you when I called at the Bomber Command last week, also to get your message through Group Captain Davis that it would not be possible to see you on Saturday last, but I am very grateful to you for the invitation to come down and see you on the subject, which I wished to discuss, and am hoping you will send me a postagram to say when I may come. I can fly down from Shawbury to Halton, as I have made arrangements to get to our various sub-stations by 'plane when there is an urgency.

Group Captain Davis suggested that I should send to you the memorandum on the subject of my scheme and I enclose it. D. Arm. D. and Air Marshal Joubert each have a copy and I have discussed it with the latter and Wing Commander Bruce of D. Arm. D. who is in charge of Gliding Weapon Development.

The subject is the attack of dams in enemy countries.

These are of varying importance, the principal being the Mohne dam in the Ruhr and this Department has given a great deal of study to their destruction.

I have a list with the particulars of the dams.

The destruction of the Mohne dam would flood the Ruhr valley and disorganize its industry.

It is probably very heavily defended, so it is desirable to attack it from a distance and from a height.

By the scheme proposed this is possible, namely by the combination of gliding weapon attack and high explosive-capacity self-propelled water-borne torpedoes or skimmers, which weapons are under active development by the Navy and have reached the stage of full size trials.

The dam is probably screened by nets and/or barges both of which the scheme proposed can defeat.

Bombs of weight to attack the dry face of the dam efficiently are now available.

Aircraft exists of a type to carry the weapons proposed for the attack of the water-face of the dam and others are now being built of a type to carry the super-bombs for attacking the dry face of the dam.

No existing weapon suffices to attack the water face, but a suitable weapon is now within clear view, thanks to the development carried out on my suggestion by this Department and the Navy.

A method is known to me of making the torpedo or skimmer, once in the water, take up a compass course, and a design exists which ensures either of these, once set upon a course at speed, maintaining that course.

/Contd.

By May 1942, the concept had been tested on a plaster model dam at the Building Research Establishment in Watford, and in July tests continued on a disused dam at Nant-y-Gro in Wales. January 1943 saw the first demonstrations using a modified Lancaster bomber. From then, the concept moved quickly from development into practice. Nevertheless, there were still questions about the viability of such a daring mission that was dependent on so many things going right, as a memorandum from Sir Arthur Harris in February 1943 made clear.

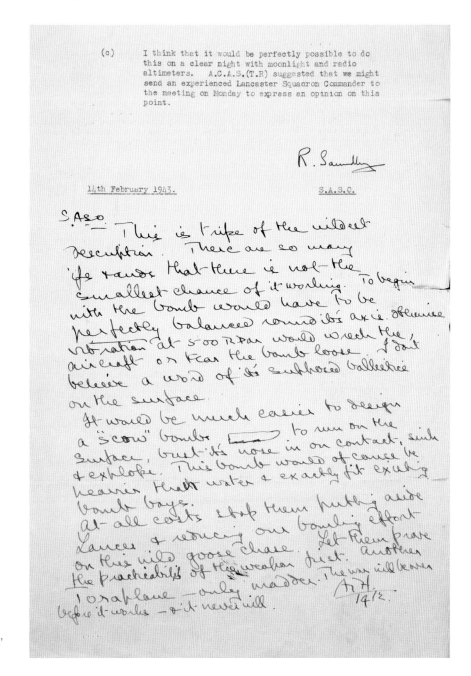

(c)   I think that it would be perfectly possible to do this on a clear night with moonlight and radio altimeters. A.C.A.S.(T.R) suggested that we might send an experienced Lancaster Squadron Commander to the meeting on Monday to express an opinion on this point.

R. Saundby

14th February 1943.   S.A.S.O.

S.A.S.O.
— This is tripe of the wildest description. There are so many 'ifs' and 'ands' that there is not the smallest chance of it working. To begin with the bomb would have to be perfectly balanced round its axis otherwise vibration at 500 R.P.M. would wreck the aircraft or tear the bomb loose. I don't believe a word of its supposed ballistics on the surface.

It would be much easier to design a "scow" bomb, [ ] to run on the surface, bust its nose in on contact, sink & explode. This bomb would of course be heavier than water & exactly fit existing bomb bays.

At all costs stop them putting aside Lancs & reducing our bombing effort on this wild goose chase. Let them prove the practicability of the weapon first. Another 1 or aeroplane — only madder. The war will be over before it works — or it never will.

A.H.
14/2.

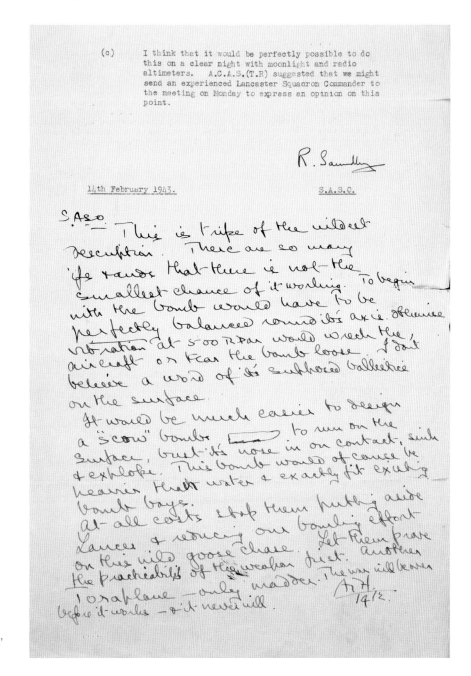
...emo from Arthur Harris
...ncerning 'bouncing bomb'
...sts, February 1943. ▶

163

The plan

Deployment of the 'bouncing bomb' involved releasing the device from an altitude of just 60ft over water and at an air speed of 240mph. To fulfil this task, the Lancaster III was developed as a modified version of the aircraft, with the dorsal gun turret and part of the ventral turret removed, along with much of the internal armouring, to reduce weight. This was essential to make space for the large bomb and the accompanying motor that provided spin to the weapon as it fell.

▲ Model tests at Nant-y-Gro July 1942.

Modified Lancaster used in the Dambusters raid, 1943. ▼

Preparations continued apace and a new squadron, 617, was formed at RAF Scampton in Lincolnshire with Wg Cdr Guy P. Gibson in command. The crews comprised men from the Royal Australian Air Force, the Royal New Zealand Air Force and the Royal Canadian Air Force, as well as the RAF.

The dams identified for the attack were located deep within Germany and the purpose of the mission was to cut off the supply of water to industry and cities essential for the German war effort. Catastrophic flooding and loss of electricity would be not insignificant by-products of the raid. An operation order, giving full details of the plan of attack, was issued in May 1943.

The attack

The 19 Lancasters were divided into three formations. No. 1 formation comprised nine aircraft with instructions to attack the Möhne; leftover ordnance would then be used to attack the Eder Dam. No. 2 formation totalled five aircraft, whose mission was to attack the Sorpe. No. 3 formation comprised a reserve, which was to take off after the first two formations and attack the main dams and the smaller Lister, Ennepe and Diemel dams.

Flying over the North Sea at a low level, they then continued for 200 miles over enemy-occupied and German territory. Along the route, one aircraft was shot down and another was forced to return to England, but the first formation reached the Möhne Dam and Guy Gibson's aircraft started the first bombing run. He was closely followed by Flt Lt John Hopgood, whose aircraft was damaged by flak and the blast from his own bomb. After five runs, the Möhne Dam was breached.

Operation *Chastise* flight paths to the dam. ▼

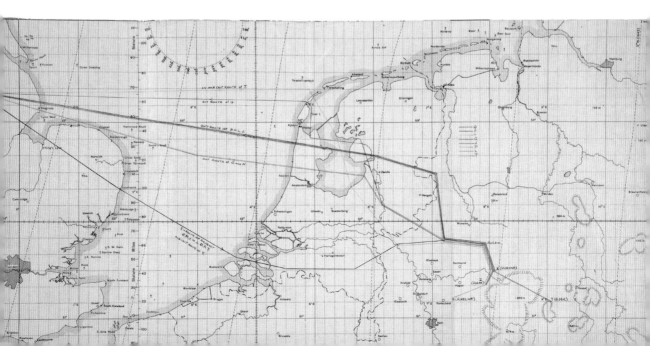

Five aircraft flew on to the Eder Dam and, using their remaining three bombs, managed to breach it. Flt Lt David Shannon made several runs at the target, successfully releasing on the seventh attempt, and the following attack by PO Les Knight ended with the breach of the dam wall. Part of the

▲ Möhne Dam breach from the ground, May 1943.

Eder Dam downstream at Kassel. ▼

difficulty of this target was the topography, which made it hard to approach the dam as intended, and this accounted for the six unsuccessful attempts by Shannon's aircraft.

The second part of the raid comprised five aircraft, which were to attack the Sorpe Dam. However, two were shot down en route, with two others damaged and forced to return. This left one remaining aircraft, and after ten attempts the bomb was successfully released and exploded against the dam. However, the Sorpe's earth construction made it particularly hard to breach and the effects of the blast were limited.

SORPE DAM
(After attack)
K 1559
Neg. No. 24689

Sorpe Dam after the attack. ▷

◀ Operation *Chastise* cypher ordering immediate attack, 15 May 1943.

Nevertheless, there was still a third phase to the attack and another bomb was released on to the Sorpe with little resulting effect. The Ennepe Dam was also hit but again without result. Two aircraft from this third wave had been lost even before they reached the targets.

The aftermath

The raid caused flooding from the breach of the Möhne and Eder dams: 330 million tons of water flowed from a breach 250ft wide and 292ft deep in the Möhne Dam, which flooded into the Ruhr district and into mines, houses and factories. Roads, railways and bridges were washed away and it has been estimated that water production fell by three-quarters. Hydroelectric

Sqn Ldr Searby,
Wg Cdr Gibson,
Sqn Ldr Ward-Hunt.

power was also lost due to damage to the dams, and two power stations were destroyed, including the Brinkhausen power station.

While the damage to the dams was quickly repaired, around 10,000 German soldiers had to be diverted for the duration of the war to guard them rather than being deployed more productively on the front line. Coal production fell in May 1943 in the aftermath of the raid by 400,000 tons and, in addition, much farmland was rendered unusable for the rest of the war and beyond by the effects of the flooding. Estimates of the numbers killed on the ground by flooding vary, but are thought to be around 1,650.

The raid cost the lives of 53 of the 133 aircrew who took part in it, a high percentage even for Bomber Command. Only 11 aircraft returned to Scampton. Those who did return were given a heroes' welcome and there is no doubt that the raid boosted morale among the British public. Guy Gibson was awarded a Victoria Cross, and 34 of the aircrew in total received decorations at Buckingham Palace.

OPERATION *CATECHISM*
The raid that destroyed the *Tirpitz*

Following Operation *Source* in September 1943 (see page 132), when the Royal Navy inflicted serious damage on the *Tirpitz*, the Royal Air Force took its turn to attack the vessel. Having been put out of action for six months by the damage inflicted by *Source*, by April 1944, the *Tirpitz* was once again afloat and the source of major anxiety for the Admiralty. Something else had to be done.

Repeated raids
An additional attack by the Fleet Air Arm in April 1944 caused further damage, killing 122 of the ship's seamen, but failed to deliver a knockout blow. In September and October 1944, the RAF had launched two raids code named *Paravane* and *Obviate*. *Paravane* involved 23 Lancasters from the RAF's

Battleship *Tirpitz*, camouflaged in Aas Fjord, Norway, 15 February 1942. ▼

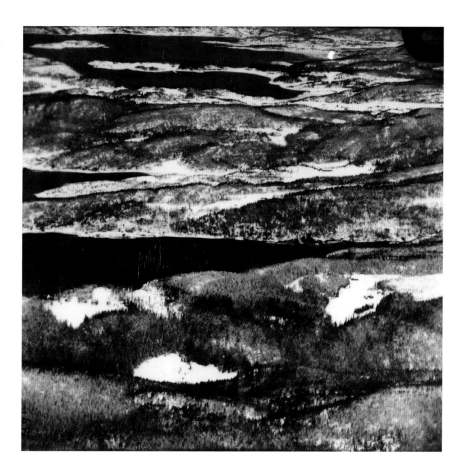

5 Group, which operated out of a base at Yagodnik in Russia, and used six short-ton Tallboy bombs to penetrate the ship's armour plating. In the event, however, they only scored one hit on the bow, with a Tallboy bomb penetrating the ship, exiting the keel and exploding on the bottom of the fjord. This caused sufficient damage to render the *Tirpitz* unseaworthy, but repairs were quick and the ship was then moved south to Tromso.

On 29 October, Operation *Obviate* was put into play and 32 Lancasters from No. 9 Squadron and No. 617 Squadron again attacked *Tirpitz*, while she was moored at the island of Haakoy, near Tromso, in a round trip of 2,252 miles. Once again, the operation was partially successful; only one of the attacking Lancasters suffered damage, all of the others returned from the mission intact, and the raid resulted in damage to the propeller shaft from a near miss, and flooding from the entry of 800 tons of water into the ship – yet it still remained afloat. It was against this backdrop that the RAF were instructed to prepare an attack, code named *Catechism*.

Picking the right moment

Up until then, the weather had proved a constant irritant in the attempts of No. 9 Squadron and No. 617 Squadron to sink the *Tirpitz*. When winds were westerly, which was the prevailing direction, Tromso was persistently obscured by cloud, thus hampering efforts. For the ninth attack on *Tirpitz*, a window of only five days of favourable weather was predicted; on 26 November, this window would effectively close since daylight would become sufficiently short.

The RAF therefore chose the morning of 12 November 1944, at 02:30, to launch the mission. The major challenge at that stage was to ensure that all of the bomber crews could keep in contact with each other. The overall commander of the raid, Gp Capt Colin Campbell McMullen, took the decision to appoint Sqn Ldr Bill Williams as squadron commander over the radio, after No. 9 Squadron's leader, Jim Bazin, did not get off the ground. Breaking radio silence was a risk, but essential if cohesion was to be maintained.

Reaching the target

The route took the procession of Lancasters through carefully identified gaps in German radar at only 1,500ft, then, when they reached the target area, they rose to the bombing altitude of 12,000–16,000ft. There were no German fighters from the nearest airfield at Bardufoss to meet them; there was apparent confusion as 18 Luftwaffe aircraft were scrambled to *Tirpitz*'s old mooring at Kaa Fjord, where she had been berthed earlier in the year. By the time they discovered their mistake, there was not enough fuel for them to complete a journey to *Tirpitz*'s new location, where the attack was unfolding.

Through a gap in the clouds, *Tirpitz* could now clearly be seen by the Lancaster pilots. Wg Cdr Willie Tait described the scene: 'She was a black shape clearly seen against the clear waters of the fjord, surrounded by the snow-covered hills, which were glowing pink in the low Arctic sun. A plume of smoke rose slowly from the big ship's funnel.' According to German accounts, the presence of such a large formation of bombers, unharried by the Luftwaffe, took the crew by surprise. It was only at 09:27 that the captain broadcast to the ship that a heavy air attack was imminent. At 09:35, the ship's main guns started firing up towards the Lancasters, with plentiful flak, though this proved ineffective against the bombers, with only one sufficiently damaged that it later had to ditch in Sweden.

The bombardment

Meanwhile, the Tallboy bombs were starting to cause serious damage to the ship. A massive piece of 'earthquake' ordnance, the Tallboy had been developed by the British aeronautical engineer Barnes Wallis (he of the 'bouncing bomb'). It measured in at 12,000lb and 21ft in length. As such, the only bomber capable of carrying it was the Lancaster, and it required a 'Stabilized Automatic Bomb Sight' to be present so that it could be targeted with pinpoint accuracy. As Sir Archibald Sinclair, the Secretary of State for Air, remarked on 15 November after the raid:

> The people of this country will take great pride in the destruction of the *Tirpitz* as an achievement of British aircraft, manned by British crews, working on a British bombsight and dropping British bombs which no other air force in the world today can carry, except the Royal Air Force. It is an astonishing development that has taken place during these five years of war in air power. If you look back at the beginning of the war, and now, in November 1944, you can carry a 12,000 pound bomb a distance of 1,200 miles to Tromso and 1,200 miles back, drop a bomb when you get there from 16,000 to 17,000 feet with an accuracy which could not have been dreamed of four to five years ago, even from a very low height.

Technological developments were clearly acknowledged even in 1944 as a powerful factor in the success of the mission.

The ordnance fell – close to the speed of sound at 750mph – in a very concentrated window of eight minutes. Several landed in the anti-torpedo nets around the ship and had the effect of cratering the seabed and shifting away the sand that was banked up around the ship in an effort to prevent her capsizing. A few were recorded to have struck the ship and ricocheted towards the beach, which would account for the enormous fractured bomb cases later retrieved from the shore. No. 617 Squadron's first bomb fell forward of the bridge and rendered the ship's services ineffective; another landed amidships and increased the ship's list to 15–20 degrees. One landed halfway down the length of the hull and although it was a near miss, it caused a huge dent 50ft long and 4ft deep down the side of the ship. The force of this turned *Tirpitz*, already listing by 60 degrees, completely over. In an indication of how quickly the raid unfolded, the captain of *Tirpitz* had given the order to abandon the lower decks at 09:50, by which point the ship was effectively finished.

▲ Aerial view of the sunken *Tirpitz*, 1945.

◄ View of the damage to the bottom of the *Tirpitz* caused by the near-miss 12,000lb bomb – a dent 50ft long and 4ft deep.

he starboard side, showing
ne armour removed and the
dent from the near-miss
2,000lb bomb. ▷

After the event

The toll on the German side was considerable: an estimated 950–1,204 sailors were lost as *Tirpitz* capsized and a rescue effort over the following days had limited success, although 82 men were freed from the upturned hull by cutting through the hull plates.

The RAF had therefore successfully achieved its aim of neutralizing Germany's biggest battleship, which had caused so much consternation at the Admiralty and to Winston Churchill himself, without *Tirpitz* having sunk or damaged any Allied shipping. Had *Tirpitz* broken out of the fjords unchallenged, she would have posed a serious threat to the Arctic convoys that supplied Russia. In this respect it was mission accomplished.

The analysis report was meticulous and provided the Air Ministry with much to confirm the effectiveness of the raid. Only a few hours afterwards, a Mosquito carried out photographic reconnaissance showing *Tirpitz* lying capsized and unsalvageable in 9 fathoms of water. Remarkably, the entire action was filmed from 16,000ft by one of the Lancasters, and it was this film, along with aerial photographs, that was used in the report of 21 November.

The success of the raid was quickly publicized and part of the film was released across Britain and the rest of the world; interest came also from the USA and the Air Ministry prepared stock details in response to media questions. Flt Lt Bruce Buckham, who was the pilot of the photographic

Lancaster of No. 463 Squadron, had had an excellent view of the action and later appeared at a press conference. His flight had taken more than 14 hours and he received a DSO; DFCs were awarded to his crew.

Many other decorations were awarded to those who had been involved in the raid itself, including a DSO for Flt Lt Robert Knights and a DFC for PO Norman Evans. Sir Archibald Sinclair, expressing his appreciation of the RAF, noted the contribution made by the aircrews and ground staff involved in the operation. Other messages of appreciation were received from Winston Churchill, President Roosevelt and Stalin – the latter because the raid freed the Arctic convoys from the menace of Germany's most powerful battleship.

When the war in Europe ended in May 1945, a number of photographs of the damage were taken from the ground. The salvage of *Tirpitz* started in 1948 and lasted a full nine years, such was the size of the vessel nicknamed 'the Beast' by Churchill.

OPERATION *CROSSBOW*
The operation against V-1 and V-2 sites in Holland, 1943–45

Operation *Crossbow* was the code name given to the Allied air operation against German V-1 and V-2 rocket launch sites in the Low Countries. In fact, it comprised a series of raids from August 1943 until May 1945 designed to target the research and development, manufacture, transportation and launch of these deadly missiles. One of the more well known of these raids was Operation *Hydra*, which occurred on the night of 17–18 August 1943 and effectively signalled the start of *Crossbow*.

German rocket development and the establishment at Peenemünde
The development of remotely controlled aircraft by Germany had started as far back as 1936 with the Argus Motoren company, but it was not until November 1939 that a proposal was made to the German Air Ministry for one that was capable of carrying a payload of 2,200lb. Thus began the V-1 rocket programme, from which the V-2 weapons subsequently developed. Known as *Vergeltungswaffen* – 'Vengeance weapons' – both the V-1 and V-2 weapons were designed for bombing London. The former had an operational range of 160 miles and the latter of 200 miles, which meant that they could be launched from Northern France and the Low Countries.

Hitler hoped that an onslaught from these new weapons would deliver victory in the war – something the British were aware of – and in December 1942 reports surfaced of testing of long-range rockets at Peenemünde on the Baltic coast.

Peenemünde was founded in 1937 and was located on a remote peninsula at Usedom for which the Air Ministry paid 750,000 Reichsmarks to the local town of Wolgast. It was here that development of rocketry began in earnest, a by-product – it is said – of the limitations imposed by the Treaty of Versailles on the development of conventional weapons. The site, when constructed,

-1 flying bomb. ▷

ormation on V-1,
eenemünde 1945. ▷

comprised experimental, research and development laboratories, workshops and a headquarters for the rocket programme. The two halves of Peenemünde comprised the Experimental Works in the east, and an airfield for test launches in the west. Intentionally, few trees were cut down so as to provide some degree of secrecy, although later aerial reconnaissance photographs by the RAF proved this deception to be fruitless.

Full-scale work on the V-1 had only really begun in 1942; the earlier work had actually taken place away from Peenemünde. However, by 1943 there

Peenemünde, 23 June
43.

were plans to produce around 2,000 of these 'flying bombs' per month, rising to 5,000 per month by the middle of 1944. Peenemünde also became the test launching site for the new rockets, which contained 2,200lb of high explosive.

The plan for Operation *Hydra*

As British concerns grew, a series of reconnaissance trips by the RAF were set up and the photographs they brought back confirmed suspicions. In December 1942, intelligence had arrived in the form of a conversation

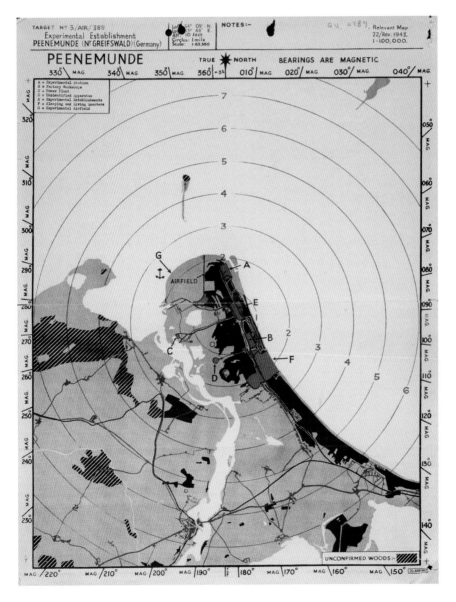

Peenemünde, 1943.

overheard by a Danish chemical engineer in Berlin about a rocket test near Swinemünde involving more than 5 tons of explosive. It was clear from prisoner of war and Polish intelligence, as well as RAF photo reconnaissance, that the rocket programme posed a huge danger to Britain.

On 29 June 1943, the Cabinet's Defence Committee (Operations) met in the Cabinet War Room where the intelligence was discussed and at length endorsed. Winston Churchill said: 'Peenemünde is … beyond the range of our radio navigation beams and … we must bomb by moonlight, although the German night fighters will be close at hand and it is too far to send our own. Nevertheless, we must attack it on the heaviest possible scale.' By 15 July, it was decided that an attack would take place at the earliest opportunity afforded by favourable weather conditions.

Bomber Command was tasked with the raid and received orders to attack three areas of the site at Peenemünde: the experimental establishment, the factory workshops and the accommodation. The last of these included a Wehrmacht barracks but unfortunately also labour camps for the foreign workers. The object was to destroy the infrastructure essential to the development of V rockets, but not necessarily the launch ramps on the airfield.

The challenges in mounting such a raid were significant. Night-time bombing was an inaccurate science and the Germans were expected to put up smokescreens. A device code named *Oboe* had been used to direct 'area bombing' with Pathfinder aircraft then able to drop markers; however, Peenemünde was beyond its effective range as the curvature of the earth interfered. H2S airborne radar sets would, though, prove to be helpful as these could be carried with the Pathfinder aircraft themselves.

The raid

Sir Arthur Harris of Bomber Command had to wait until Tuesday 17 August for favourable meteorological and lunar conditions to mount the raid. A lunar period started on 11 August and by the 17th there would be a full or near full moon to increase visibility of targets. Better still, weather conditions would be clear. The raid would comprise 324 Lancasters, 218 Halifaxes and 54 Stirling aircraft. Crews were not informed of the real reason for the raid; the site was described as being for German radar development. A route that took the aircraft over the sea and German-occupied Denmark was planned – far preferable than flying over Germany itself.

At 12:10 British time the first 'red spot fire' was started; these were ignited at 3,000ft over the target and burned for ten minutes on reaching the ground. A minute later, 16 blind markers dropped target indicators and parachute flares that would provide illumination for visual markers. Just before Zero Hour – the start of the raid – the visual markers then showed the exact aiming points with yellow target indicators. An error in the first part of the marking meant that there was confusion among the following aircraft about where to release their target indicators, but this was corrected by the visual markers and the raid was able to proceed, albeit at the cost of several minutes during which the situation for the main bombing force was unclear.

The bombs were to be released from around 8,000ft; this was comparatively low given that 19,000ft was the normal altitude for raids. It was anticipated that there would be much flak at that level, yet crews reported that the German defences were seriously ineffective. During the entire process of marking the area with flares, as well as the first phase of the raid, the RAF went completely unchallenged by the Luftwaffe. The flak was slow to open up, and only one searchlight was in use. Sgt E.H. Burgess of No. 78 Squadron reported that the raid was like being 'on a joyride'.

Flt Sgt W.L. Combs of No. 15 Squadron described the intensity of the raid:

> The target area was an incandescent mass as we flew over on our bombing run…
> Not on any bombing attack have I experienced such a buffeting as we received
> over the target but I suspect this was caused mainly by blast from bomb explosions
> on the ground only 6,000 feet below rather than nearby flak bursts.

The first phase of the raid ended after aircraft received light flak at around 12:27. These included a Halifax of No. 158 Squadron, whose mid-upper gunner Sgt J.E.T. Pearson recalled the resulting flames around the starboard engine that eventually resulted in the first RAF deaths of the raid: Flt Sgt Caldwell and four other crew.

The second part of the raid commenced at 12:31 and comprised RAF 1 Group, whose target was the V-2 production works – as opposed to 3 & 4 Group, which had spearheaded the attack in the first phase by attacking the accommodation areas. To begin with, however, a complex and hitherto unattempted operation had to be put in place to shift the marking from the first area to the new target. This was successfully accomplished by the master bomber and the actions of Sqn Ldr J. Lofthouse of No. 7 Squadron, who placed markers directly over the two production buildings that had been identified as targets. The phase lasted for just 11 minutes and was over by 12:42. In all, more than 124 bombers released 480 tons of high explosive and 40 tons of incendiaries, which was described by Sgt J.J. Minguy, No. 101 Squadron: 'On the ground, everything was going up and burning as it isn't possible. This was a mixture of flashes from the ground defences, which seemed to increase their firing in the same measure as we were raining them with bombs, and of explosions which were all the more spectacular one from the other.' Sgt A.C. Farmer, No. 12 Squadron, described the sensation as being like 'riding a car across a ploughed field.'

The third wave hit the experimental works using aircraft from Nos 4 & 5 Squadron, causing serious damage to the laboratory and office. This was arguably the most important part of the mission. Many Halifax and Lancaster bombers, however, flew past the target, due to smoke and inaccurately 'shifted' green markers, and their ordnance fell 2,000 yards away on the concentration camp site. Thus concluded Operation *Hydra*.

After the raid

The following morning, a Mosquito reconnaissance flew over Peenemünde and returned with photographs that showed the damage caused, including buildings destroyed and heavily cratered ground. Some 1,795 tons of ordnance had been released over Peenemünde and as well as the physical damage, a number of staff on the ground had been killed, including Dr Thiel and Chief Engineer Walther; one of the aims of the raid was undoubtedly to kill as many scientists, engineers and researchers as possible so as to disrupt the rocket programme.

First impressions of the damage from aerial photographs were, however, misleading. It did not take long for many of the buildings to be repaired or replaced, and these were soon functioning again. It certainly was not the decisive knock-out blow that the RAF hoped it would be. The most critical parts of the Experimental Works and Production Works were not particularly heavily damaged.

Furthermore, another purpose of the raid had been to destroy important documents that were relied upon for weapons development, but these too largely escaped the bombing since the Germans had a policy of dispersing such vital documents. As for the accommodation portion of the site that was heavily bombed, it appeared that the level of damage to buildings disguised the fact that only two scientists were killed – the main target of the raid. By contrast, high casualties were suffered by Polish and other foreign workers housed in the small camp.

Many of these failures can be attributed to the extreme difficulty in accurately marking targets throughout the raid during night-time conditions, resulting in bombs falling on the wrong targets or missing altogether. The RAF lost 40 bombers during the raid, along with 290 aircrew. The list of those who never returned included men from Canada, Australia, the USA and New Zealand, along with 167 British aircrew.

Peenemünde V-2 site before and after the attack on 17–18 August 1943. ▼

Portion Enlarged.

In light of these statistics and the fact that the complete destruction of Peenemünde had not been achieved, the raid was certainly not a full success. Nevertheless, the German assessment by Joseph Goebbels concluded that the missile programme was set back by six to eight weeks by the raid. Furthermore, Dr Thiel, who had been killed during the raid, was the propulsion specialist working on the Wasserfall anti-aircraft rocket and the more powerful A9 rocket, which would have put the whole of Britain within range. Neither of these weapons was subsequently produced, although the war ended too soon in any case for this to have happened. If the delay of eight weeks is factored into the V-2 programme, that would suggest that the RAF had been able to reduce by more than 700 the number of rockets eventually fired.

ecial Projectiles Operations
oup, V-2 rocket firing trials,
May 1945–18 October
45. ▷

Postscript

In the event, the development of missiles was withdrawn from Peenemünde in October 1943 although the site continued to be used for other purposes. Three raids by the US 8th Air Force took place on 18 July, 4 August and 25 August 1944 to disrupt suspected production of hydrogen peroxide – a key component of rockets. The first V-1 flying bombs landed on London on 12 June 1944, but accuracy was poor and the RAF developed techniques to deflect the bombs from their trajectory. Nevertheless, the V-1 and V-2 rockets caused great damage in London and south-east England and launches only stopped when the launch sites, which had been heavily targeted by the RAF and US Air Force, were overrun by the Allies as they pushed towards Germany in 1945.

▲ V-1 incident, Aldwych, London, 30 June 1944.

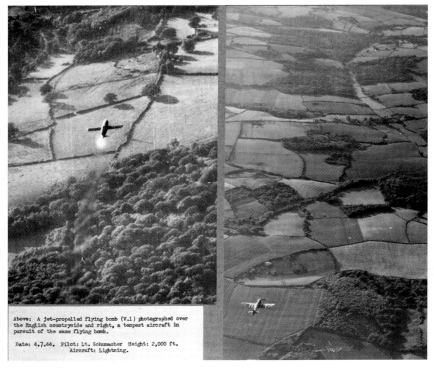

Above: A jet-propelled flying bomb (V.1) photographed over the English countryside and right, a tempest aircraft in pursuit of the same flying bomb.

Date: 4.7.44. Pilot: Lt. Schumacher Height: 2,000 ft.
Aircraft: Lightning.

◀ V-1 chase, 4 July 1944.

Operation *Crossbow* Ski
sites confirmed in France,
1943–44. ▶

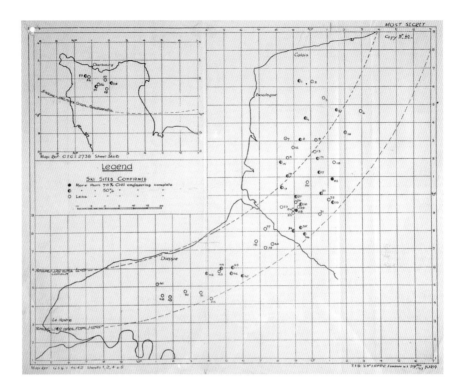

First V-2 strike, Staveley
Road, Chiswick, London,
8–9 September 1944. ▼

OPERATION *MINCEMEAT*
A dead man spreads misinformation to German forces, 1943

In the run-up to D-Day, a number of deception operations were carried out by British intelligence to deceive the Germans as to the time and location of the Allied landings. One of the most famous, ingenuous and macabre of these was Operation *Mincemeat* – the purpose of which was to convince the Germans that the Allies' main military thrust in the Mediterranean would be through the Balkans, rather than their true objective: the island of Sicily.

The file on Operation *Mincemeat*. ▼

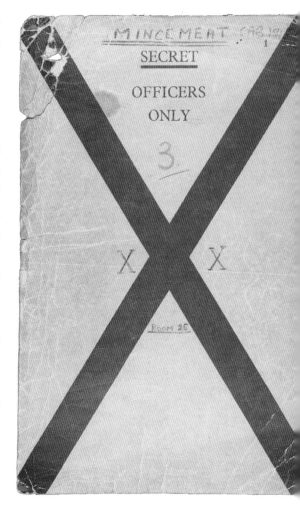

The plan is hatched

The deception plan relied on convincing the Germans that they had accidentally stumbled across secret British papers. While the idea of supplying false information to the enemy is a classic example of the dark arts employed by the secret services, its successful execution in wartime presented a host of problems. A variety of scenarios were explored, the most plausible – initially code named Operation *Trojan Horse* – relied on the use of a dead body to facilitate the transfer of secret documents into enemy hands.

The initial plan for the operation was drawn up by Charles Cholmondeley, a 25-year-old officer in the Royal Air Force temporarily seconded to the Security Service (MI5). The scheme involved obtaining a recently deceased corpse from a hospital morgue. The body would then be dressed

HW 20/546

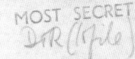

REFERENCE SHEET.

From. Lt. Cdr. Montagu, R.N.V.R. N.I.D. 12.

To.   Frank Birch, Esq. (for Cdr Travis)

Date. 30th April, 1943.

Arrangements have been made to plant on the Germans documents which are intended to lead them to believe that we are going to attack in certain places in the Mediterranean area and that other places are to be used by us as cover targets to confuse the enemy.

2.   The means of doing this is a document purporting to be a letter from V.C.I.G.S. to General Alexander and it is accompanied by letters from C.C.O. to Admiral Cunningham and to General Eisenhower. It is hoped the Germans will believe that these documents were lost in an air crash.

3.   If mention of this information should be put out by the enemy in Special Intelligence there could be no harm in this having the usual distribution and, in fact, that would be the most satisfactory course. 4If, however, the enemy, or even the Spaniards, state that these facts have been learnt from documents lost in an air crash, or from the letters passing between the people mentioned above or any similar identification of the source different considerations prevail. A receipt of such Special Intelligence by those normally receiving it in this country and the Mediterranean and Middle East would probably result in a "flap" and numerous enquiries on security grounds as to what has been lost and how it came to be lost.

5.5.   In these circumstances I hope that you could arrange that if a message or messages on the lines indicated in the last preceding paragraph are received, distribution could be prevented and that only "C" and myself are notified. I will undertake to see that the other Ministries

/are

are informed and make immediate arrangements for the necessary information to be passed to those in the know in the Middle East and Mediterranean: if the information is routed through those in the know the information will be available there and the "flap" will be prevented.

Lt. Cdr., R.N.V.R.

op-secret documents
utlining the details of
peration *Mincemeat.* ▶

189

in military uniform, handcuffed to a briefcase carrying military plans, transported overseas and finally washed up on a beach in enemy-occupied territory where it would be found and handed over to the relevant authorities.

The scheme relied on the Germans discovering the plans, copying them and then handing the papers and body back to the British without any evidence that the security of the documents had been compromised. It also involved other significant challenges: first, how to obtain a suitable cadaver that would convince the Germans that the body had recently died in an accident at sea; and second, how to transport the corpse overseas without it deteriorating, then drop it in the water in the right location so that it would be washed up on the beach and not taken out to sea – all without being detected.

Since the corpse was to be dropped at sea, the deception, now known as Operation *Mincemeat*, was placed under the control of Lt Cdr Ewen Montagu of Naval Intelligence. The main details of the operation were finalized in January 1943 and hinged on convincing the Germans that the body was that of a passenger aboard a military plane that had crashed off the Spanish coast. To bolster the deception, the body was handcuffed to a briefcase containing a 'Personal and Most Secret' letter from the Vice Chief of the Imperial General Staff, Lt Gen Archibald Nye to the Commander of British Forces in the Middle East, Gen Harold Alexander, that outlined Allied intentions in Southern Europe. The letter confirmed that American and British forces stationed in North Africa planned to cross the Mediterranean to launch an attack on German-held Greece and Sardinia and that an attack on Sicily was part of a deception operation designed to fool the Germans as to the Allies' true intentions.

Preparing the cadaver

The plan received the approval of the chiefs-of-staff and the cadaver of a 34-year-old man was discreetly obtained from St Stephen's Hospital, Fulham, London. The body was that of a labourer of no fixed abode called Glyndwr Michael who had recently committed suicide by swallowing phosphorus rat poison. In the absence of an elaborate post-mortem, his death would be consistent with an air crash at sea.

The body was given the false identity of Maj Martin, an officer in the Royal Marines. To further strengthen the deception, it was dressed in military uniform and a variety of items were placed in the pockets to build up a backstory.

e false ID card created for
e fictitious Maj Martin. ▶

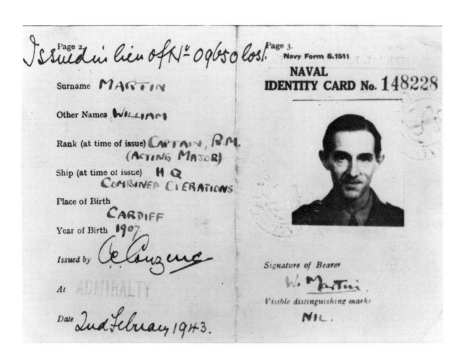

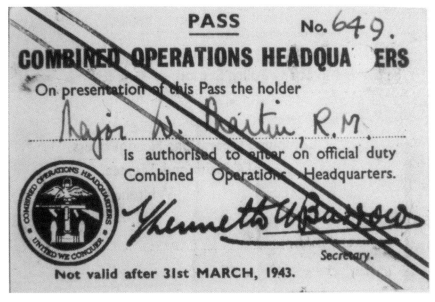

aj Martin's forged Combined
perations pass. ▶

These included: a demand for settlement of a £79 19s 2d overdraft from Lloyds bank; a letter from his fiancée; and two theatre tickets for a variety show at the Prince of Wales Theatre starring the music-hall comedian Sid Field. The fake love letter from 'Pam', his fiancée, was created by two women at MI5; the letter itself (and another dated Wednesday 21 April) was written by

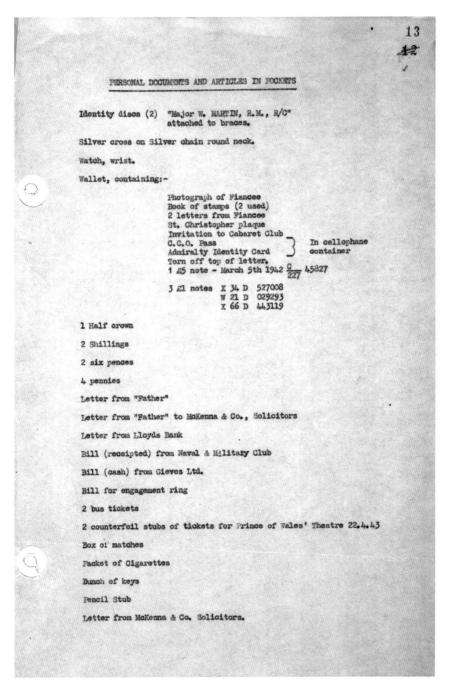

13

PERSONAL DOCUMENTS AND ARTICLES IN POCKETS

Identity discs (2)   "Major W. MARTIN, R.M., R/C"
                           attached to braces.

Silver cross on Silver chain round neck.

Watch, wrist.

Wallet, containing:-

               Photograph of Fiancee
               Book of stamps (2 used)
               2 letters from Fiancee
               St. Christopher plaque
               Invitation to Cabaret Club
               C.C.O. Pass   In cellophane
               Admiralty Identity Card   container
               Torn off top of letter.
               1 £5 note - March 5th 1942 $\frac{C}{227}$ 45827

               3 £1 notes X 34 D 527008
                             W 21 D 029293
                             X 66 D 443119

1 Half crown

2 Shillings

2 six pences

4 pennies

Letter from "Father"

Letter from "Father" to McKenna & Co., Solicitors

Letter from Lloyds Bank

Bill (receipted) from Naval & Military Club

Bill (cash) from Gieves Ltd.

Bill for engagement ring

2 bus tickets

2 counterfoil stubs of tickets for Prince of Wales' Theatre 22.4.43

Box of matches

Packet of Cigarettes

Bunch of keys

Pencil Stub

Letter from McKenna & Co. Solicitors.

Hester Leggett, head of the secretarial team at MI5, and the accompanying photograph was provided by Jean Leslie, a young MI5 secretary. To further the illusion, a receipt from a New Bond Street jeweller for an engagement ring was added to Martin's wallet.

...rsonal effects that were planted [?] the body. ▷

(...elow and overleaf) More planted ...rrespondence left on the body.

21st April,
1 9 4 3.

Dear Admiral of the Fleet,

I promised V.C.I.G.S. that Major Martin would
arrange with you for the onward transmission of a
letter he has with him for General Alexander. It is
very urgent and very "hot" and as there are some
remarks in it that could not be seen by others in the
War Office, it could not go by signal. I feel sure
that you will see that it goes on safely and without
delay.

I think you will find Martin the man you want.
He is quiet and shy at first, but he really knows his
stuff. He was more accurate than some of us about the
probable run of events at Dieppe and he has been well
in on the experiments with the latest barges and
equipment which took place up in Scotland.

Let me have him back, please, as soon as the
assault is over. He might bring some sardines with him -
they are "on points" here!

yours sincerely

Louis Mountbatten

Admiral of the Fleet Sir A.B. Cunningham, G.C.B.,D.S.O.,
Commander in Chief Mediterranean,
Allied Force H.Q.,
Algiers.

Positioning the cadaver

The problem of preserving the body prior to its release in the sea was solved by packing it in dry ice and placing it in an air-tight metal container from which most of the oxygen had been removed. The container was then transported 400 miles from London to Greenock dock in Scotland, where it was loaded aboard the British submarine HMS *Seraph* under the command of Lt Bill Jewell, who had previous experience of undertaking classified missions having secretly transported Gen Eisenhower's deputy, Gen Mark Clark, to Algeria for covert talks with local French commanders.

To conceal from the crew the fact that there was a dead body on board, the container

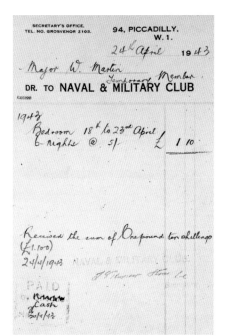

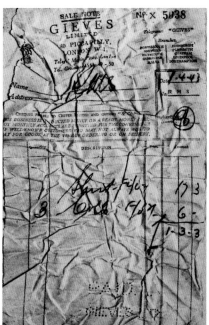

was labelled 'Handle with Care – Optical Instruments – For Special FOS [Flag Officer Submarines] Shipment'. On 19 April 1943, the *Seraph* and her gruesome cargo slowly slipped its moorings and set sail for Spanish waters.

◀ The canister in which the body was transported.

MOST SECRET

From The Commanding Officer, H.M. Submarine "SERAPH".

Date: 30th April, 1943.

To Director of Naval Intelligence.

Copy to F.O.S.

(for Lt. Cdr. The Hon. E.E.S. Montagu,R.N.V.R.) personal.

OPERATION MINCEMEAT

Weather: The wind was variable altering between SW and SE. force 2.
It was expected that the sea breeze would spring up in the
morning, close inshore, as it had on the previous morning
in similar conditions.
Sea and swell - 2.0. - Sky overcast with very low clouds -
visibility was patchy, 1 to 2 miles - Barometer 1016.

2. **Fishing boats:** A large number of small fishing boats were working in
the bay. The closest was left, about a mile off,
and it is not thought that the submarine was observed
by them.

3. **Operation:** The time of 0430 was chosen as being the nearest to Low Water
Lisbon, (0731) which would allow the submarine to be well
clear by dawn. The Cannister was opened at 0415 and the body
extracted. The blanket was opened up and the body examined. The
brief case was found to be securely attached. The face was heavily
tanned and the whole of the lower half from the eyes down covered
with mould. The skin had started to break away on the nose and
cheek bones. The body was very high. The Mae West was blown up
very hard and no further air was needed. The body was placed in
the water at 0430 in a position 148° Portil Pillar 1.3 miles
approximately eight cables from the beach and started to drift
inshore. This was aided by the wash of the screws going full
speed astern. The rubber dinghy was placed in the water blown
up and upside down about half a mile further south of this
position. The submarine then withdrew to seaward and the
cannister, filled with water, and containing the blanket, tapes
and also the rubber dinghy's container was pushed over the side in
position 36°37'30 North 07°18'00 West in 310 fathoms of water by
sounding machine. The container would not at first submerge but
after being riddled by fire from Vickers gun and also .455 revolver
at very short range was seen to sink.
Signal reporting operation complete was passed at 0715.
A sample of the water close inshore is attached.

N. L. A. JEWELL.

Lieutenant-in-Command.

The submarine's destination was Huelva, a port city in south-western Spain, at the mouth of the Odiel and Tinto rivers. On 30 April, the *Seraph* and its cargo reached its destination and surfaced a mile from the coast under the cover of darkness. The canister containing Maj Martin's body was then opened and the body examined. The briefcase was found to be securely attached. The face was discoloured and the whole of the lower half from the eyes down was covered with mould.

The body was placed in the water at 04:30 and began to drift ashore, aided by the gentle wash of the submarine's propeller. The *Seraph* then sailed south for a mile, where a rubber dinghy was inflated and placed in the water upside down. The submarine then withdrew. At 07:15, Lt Jewell sent a short wireless message to the Admiralty in London: 'Mincemeat Completed'.

Laying the paper trail

As planned, the body was eventually washed up on the shore and discovered by a fisherman who informed the local police and port authorities. It was taken to the morgue, where a doctor certified that death was due to asphyxiation through immersion in the sea while still alive. The personal effects, including the briefcase, were then removed and the body buried in a Huelva cemetery with full military honours at noon on 2 May. The German intelligence network in Spain was informed of the incident and made copies of all the documents contained in the briefcase before they returned them to Capt Alan Hillgarth, the British naval attaché in Madrid.

The copied documents were next taken to Berlin by Wilhelm Leissner, the wartime head of Abwehr operations in Spain. For the deception to work, the Germans needed to be sure that they had gained access to the papers undetected and that the British had no reason to suspect that the security of the documents had been compromised. To confirm this, an uncoded message was sent to Hillgarth via naval cable directing him to thank the Spanish naval authorities for their help in safeguarding the documents and for their prompt return. At the same time, Hillgarth received a secret coded message via diplomatic channels that confirmed that the letters had been opened, copied and then placed back into their envelopes. The bogus plan for the Allied invasion of Greece and Sardinia was now in German hands.

To provide further credence to the story, the death of Maj Martin following a plane crash was announced in *The Times.* By good fortune, his name appeared in a list of persons mainly killed in accidents. A report of the incident was sent personally to Adm Dönitz, and concluded that 'the genuineness of the documents is above suspicion' and that 'the enemy is unlikely to know that they have been captured or to start their operations earlier than they had intended'. The grave at Huelva also received a wreath and a card from Maj Martin's parents and grieving fiancée Pam, thanking the staff at the British Consulate for all their help and assistance in arranging the funeral and returning Maj Martin's personal items to the family.

The Germans swallow the story

Conclusive confirmation that the Germans had obtained the information from the letters came on 14 May when a German communication was decrypted at Bletchley Park, the top-secret home of Britain's codebreakers during World War II. This stated that the Allied invasion was to be in the Balkans, with a deception operation planned in Sicily. A cable was immediately dispatched to Winston Churchill who was then in the USA, by Brig Leslie Hollis, Secretary to the Chiefs-of-Staff Committee. It consisted of only three words: 'Mincemeat Swallowed Whole'.

German confidence in the veracity of the captured plans was reinforced by rumours and misinformation spread by the British and picked up by Turkish intelligence that the Allies were preparing to advance into the Balkans via Greece. This view was supported by the stationing of the British 12th Army in the eastern Mediterranean, consisting of 12 fictitious divisions, and the distribution of Greek maps to Allied forces. It was time to put the next part of the plan into action.

Operation *Husky*

The plan for the invasion of Sicily had been agreed at the Casablanca conference in January 1943, attended by Prime Minister Churchill, President Franklin D. Roosevelt and Gen Charles de Gaulle. Operation *Husky*, as the scheme became known, entailed an amphibious assault by 180,000 Allied troops along 100 miles of coastline on the island's southern flank, supported by naval gunfire and close air support.

Operation *Husky* began on 9 July 1943 and was the first major Allied assault on German-occupied Europe. The success of Operation *Mincemeat* meant that when the Allies landed in Sicily, they were met by just two German divisions under the command of Gen Hans Hube. The battle-hardened 1st Panzer Division was transferred from France to Salonika with two panzer divisions moved to the Balkans from the Eastern Front. German torpedo boats were also moved from Sicily to the Greek islands in preparation for the expected Allied attack. No measures were taken to reinforce the island, with German troops in the Balkans waiting in vain to repel an attack that never materialized.

The British post-war top-secret report on the operation concluded that there was no doubt that Operation *Mincemeat* succeeded in achieving the desired effect of dispersing the German effort to defend the island. It was also believed that the deception was largely responsible for the fact that the east end of Sicily, where troops landed, was much less defended than the west end of the island nearest Sardinia. The battle for Sicily lasted until 17 August and paved the way for the Allied invasion of Italy. In July, the Italian leader Benito Mussolini was deposed and a new provisional government established under Mshl Pietro Badoglio. The liberation of Europe had begun.

The story lives on

After the war, the broad outline of the story was described in *Operation Heartbreak*, a 1950 novel written by the wartime Minister of Information and Ambassador to France Alfred Duff Cooper. Following the publication, Ewen Montagu, who planned and carried out Operation *Mincemeat*, approached the government for permission to publish his own account of the operation. Initially this was refused, but when it was discovered that the investigative journalist Ian Colvin had visited Spain and was getting close to unearthing the truth, Montagu was allowed to put out his version as a spoiler, under the heading 'The Man Who Never Was'. The first instalment of the story appeared in the *Sunday Express* on 1 February 1953 and was followed a month later by a book that became a bestseller. Montagu's work formed the basis for a 1956 film *The Man Who Never Was*, starring Clifton Webb and Gloria Grahame.

In 1997, the headstone at grave number 1886 at Huelva cemetery was inscribed with the following words: 'Glyndwr Michael, served as Maj William Martin, RN'. The grave is now cared for by the Commonwealth War Graves Commission.

OPERATION *TOTALISE*
The Battle of the Falaise Pocket, 1944

Occurring during the later stages of Operation *Overlord* – the Allied forces' landing on the beaches of Normandy in the summer of 1944 – the aim of Operation *Totalise* was for Allied troops of the Canadian 1st Army to penetrate German defences south of Caen and capture the high ground north of the

(Below and overleaf) Maps showing the situation in Normandy before Operation *Totalise*. ▼

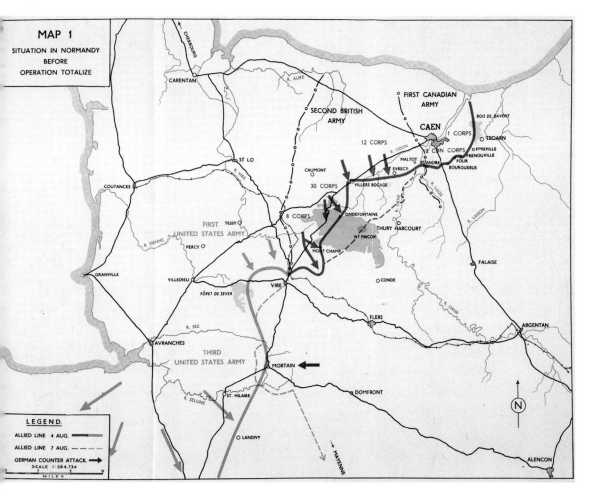

MAP 1

SITUATION IN NORMANDY
BEFORE
OPERATION TOTALIZE

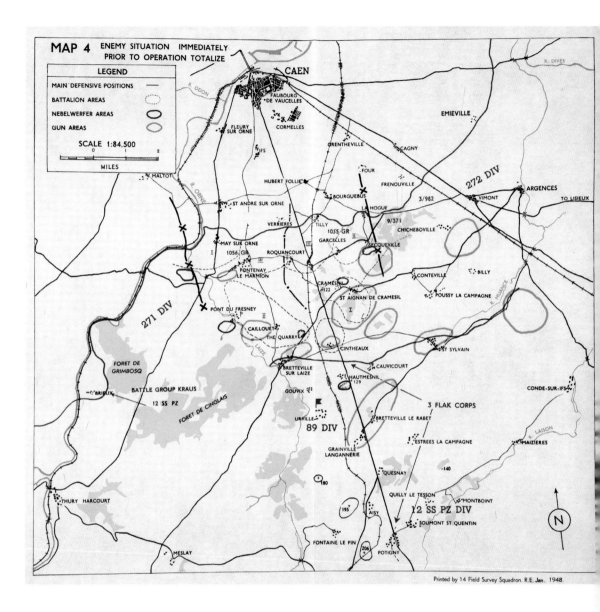

MAP 4 ENEMY SITUATION IMMEDIATELY
PRIOR TO OPERATION TOTALIZE

LEGEND

MAIN DEFENSIVE POSITIONS

BATTALION AREAS

NEBELWERFER AREAS

GUN AREAS

SCALE 1:84,500

MILES

Printed by 14 Field Survey Squadron. R.E. Jan. 1948.

city of Falaise. If successful, it was hoped that this strategy would collapse
the German front and cut off any means of retreat.

Background to Operation *Totalise*

The success of the Allied forces' landing on the beaches of Normandy is
often regarded as the turning point of World War II. It began with Allied
bombardment on 6 June 1944, which was intended to support hundreds of
landing craft full of British, American and Canadian forces who were preparing
to invade France by first breaking through the German coastal fortifications

on the Normandy coast and then by pushing inland to liberate occupied Europe. The subsequent Battle of Normandy has since been described as one of the greatest military clashes of all time.

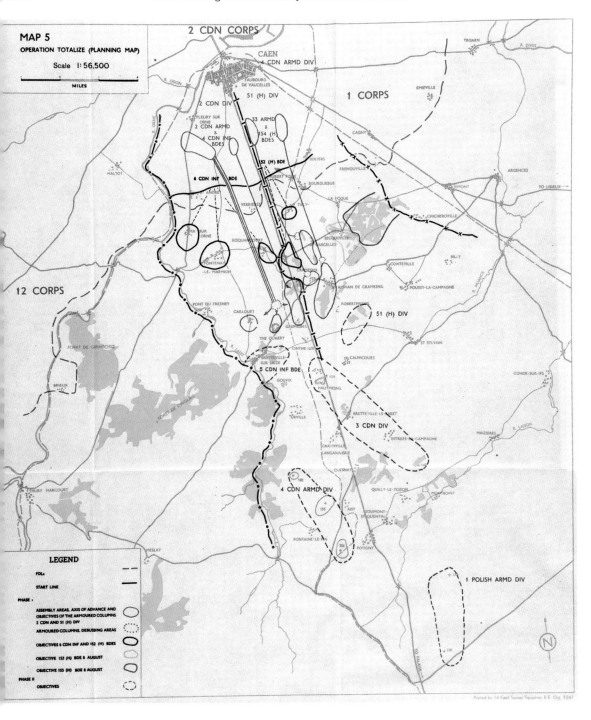

Planning map for Operation Totalise. ▼

MAP 5

OPERATION TOTALIZE (PLANNING MAP)

Scale 1:56,500

MILES

2 CDN CORPS

CAEN
4 CDN ARMD DIV

1 CORPS

51 (H) DIV

FLEURY SUR ORNE
2 CDN ARMD & 4 CDN INF BDES

33 ARMD & 154 (H) BDES

152 (H) BDE

6 CDN INF BDE

12 CORPS

51 (H) DIV

THE QUARRY

5 CDN INF BDE

3 CDN DIV

4 CDN ARMD DIV

1 POLISH ARMD DIV

LEGEND

FDLs

START LINE

PHASE I

ASSEMBLY AREAS, AXIS OF ADVANCE AND OBJECTIVES OF THE ARMOURED COLUMNS 2 CDN AND 51 (H) DIV

ARMOURED COLUMNS, DEBUSSING AREAS

OBJECTIVES 6 CDN INF AND 152 (H) BDES

OBJECTIVE 152 (H) BDE 8 AUGUST

OBJECTIVE 153 (H) BDE 8 AUGUST

PHASE II

OBJECTIVES

Printed by 14 Field Survey Squadron R.E. Oct. 1947

Commanded by FM Montgomery, on 25 July, the Allied breakout from the Normandy beachhead they had earlier secured was launched. In what became known as the Battle of the Falaise Pocket, it was this action that ultimately enabled the Allied forces to push through France and into Germany, Belgium and Holland.

The fire plan for Operation *Totalise*. ▼

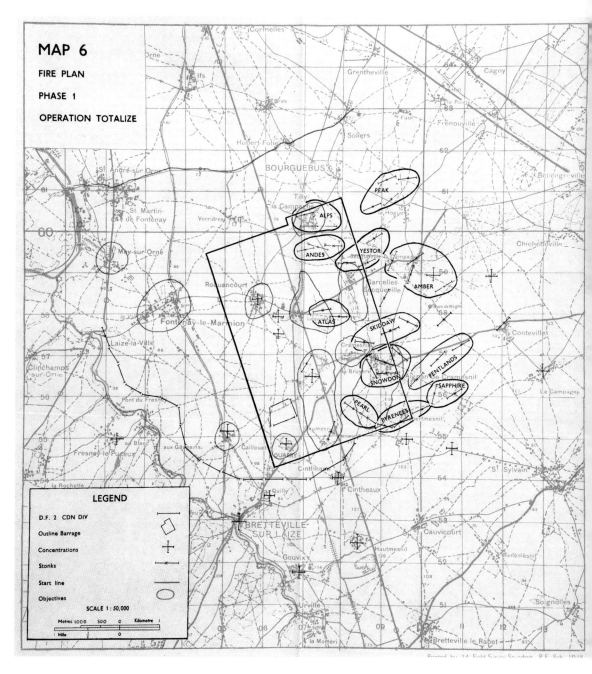

View over bombed Caen, June 1944.

Falaise itself is located in the Calvados region of Normandy – famous as the birthplace of William the Conqueror – while the 'pocket' was an area of 7 square miles surrounding the small towns of Trun, Chambois and Coudehard. A scene of undulating open country, small valleys and steep hills,

Marketplace covered by snipers, Caen, 9 July 1944. ▶

it was here that the Americans, Canadians and Polish forces found themselves fighting to seal the pocket and entrap the German 7th Division.

International cooperation

Montgomery's aim was to deliver a major attack towards Falaise on the eastern flank of the German position. The Canadians had recently brought in the 4th Armoured Division to join the 2nd and 3rd Infantry Divisions. With the addition of the Free French 2nd and Polish 1st Divisions, which now formed part of the Canadian 1st Army, they were to drive south-east of Caen to gain as much ground as possible in the direction of Falaise, to place themselves behind the enemy, who were facing the British 2nd Army. The intention was to continue to wear down the enemy formations in this sector.

Elsewhere, considerable advances were being made: Vire had been taken by the US 29th Infantry Division; the British had control of the high ground at Mont Pinçon; and British XII Corps had secured the bridgehead over

▲ British troops in Rue Basse Caen, 9 July 1944.

◀ Organization Todt, Promenade du Fort, Caen, 10 July 1944.

British soldier in Caen, 1944. ▶

Damaged buildings, Aunay-sur-Odon, Caen, France 1944. ▶

the River Orne to the north of Thury Harcourt. The Canadian II Corps had been fighting in the Caen sector since 11 July and had seen bitter action during Operation *Goodwood* between 18 and 21 July. By the end of *Goodwood*, on 25 July 1944, the Canadians had finally taken Caen, as well as taking part in major and minor missions, patrolling and firefighting in order to retain a strong position east of the Orne.

As with the D-Day landings, the closing of the Falaise pocket was an Allied operation in which the commanders from Allied armies were responsible for bringing soldiers from Canada, Britain, Poland and the USA together for one operation. The deployment of combined Allied modern artillery in the field, capable of being used in all weathers, delivered effective results, despite American and British tanks being technically inferior to those of the Germans.

Gen Omar Bradley, leading the recently initiated American 12th Army, conceived the idea of encircling the German Army from the south, through Alençon, Argentan, Mortain and Flers. The town of Argentan, straddling the

6th US Armoured Division at Lessay, 28 July 1944. ▼

roads that the Germans needed to control to have an escape route to the east and north-east, was a key objective in developing the encirclement.

The drive south

On 7 August, the Canadians opened up a new and commanding drive south. Operation *Totalise* became the first kind of warfare where the infantry were carried in armoured vehicles, formed closely behind heavily protected armoured vehicles. However, the operation was not a total success; the British Columbia Regiment suffered a loss of 47 tanks after it strayed into the Hitler Youth division, who surrounded the Canadians and cut them off. Two companies from Algonquin Infantry Regiment also suffered heavy casualties. Despite this, the Allied armoured divisions succeeded in their attempt to push towards Falaise.

For the Germans, the situation was becoming increasingly grave. FM Günther von Kluge, Supreme Commander West, was aware of the danger of encirclement; the number of tanks in the German panzer divisions were in decline and the strength of the Luftwaffe was weakening. To make matters worse, Operation *Luttich* on 8 August had failed, resulting in further depletion of German tanks. Kluge therefore speedily pressed on with his plan of defence. Realizing that holding Alençon was key, he concentrated four divisions east of Mortain and brought in remnants of the 9th and 116th Panzer Divisions to defend Alençon.

In the American camp, meanwhile, Gen Bradley ordered Gen George Patton not to advance beyond Argentan, inadvertently delaying the complete victory of the Battle of Normandy, in what many believe to be an error of judgement. Senior Allied generals' indecision and inability to resolve skirmishes are often blamed for the loss of the opportunity for a more decisive victory.

Back in the German lines, while on his way to Nécy, halfway between Argentan and Falaise, an Allied bomber attacked Kluge's convoy. Kluge managed to escape injury, but was forced to go undercover. Hitler, anxious to know Kluge's whereabouts, was convinced that he had planned to surrender his divisions and hand himself over to the Allies. After Kluge reappeared, therefore, Hitler ordered him to be replaced by FM Walter Model, one of the Führer's favourites. In his last message from his dwindling battlefield before he was replaced, Kluge issued orders for a withdrawal. This was no mean feat, since roads were impassable, tanks had no fuel and the infantry was exhausted, hungry and battle weary. Montgomery and Bradley made the decision to use all resources available to close the Falaise Gap.

On 13 August, a French patrol entered Argentan only 13 miles south-east of Falaise. Operation *Tractable* was launched a day later, bringing together the 3rd Canadian Infantry, Canadian 4th Armoured Division and the Polish 1st Armoured Division. Hundreds of armoured vehicles gathered in the undulating Orne Valley, poised to close the Falaise Gap.

The role of Polish forces

The soldiers of Poland's army-in-exile formed two divisions. The II Corps was made up of prisoners of war who had been taken by the Soviets then released from imprisonment and forced labour in July 1942. Freed from the Lubyanka

Map showing the situation at last light on 8 August. ▼

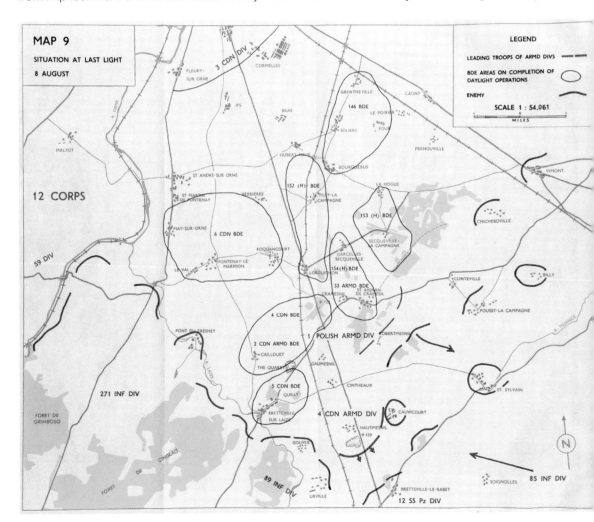

German Panzers: Tiger (right) and Panther (below). ▶

prison, Gen Władysław Anders was charged by Gen Władysław Sikorski to gather and lead the newly formed corps to battle in the Western Desert and its final battle for Monte Cassino in Italy. The I Corps was made up of soldiers who, on orders, had escaped from Poland by any means, so as to be able to re-form its army in France. Following the fall of Paris, the Poles found themselves on British soil, where Polish pilots were deployed to squadrons of Fighter Command, while soldiers were tasked with the coastal defence duties in Scotland. The British Army had planned to bring the Polish soldiers up to full fighting capacity, probably as infantry battalions, but the Poles had other ideas. Among the soldiers were experienced cavalrymen eager to retrain in the most modern of combats. Gen Sikorski therefore pushed the British for the formation of an armoured division, and chose Gen Stanisław Maczek to lead the Polish 1st Armoured Division. This was formed in Scotland in February 1942 and fought with the Canadian 1st Army during the Battle of Normandy.

The Polish 1st Armoured Division, meanwhile, landed at Arromanches on 31 July 1944. The timing was fortuitous since as Gen Maczek's army prepared the way for their long-awaited invasion and a chance to return to their homeland, Gen Bor Komorowski, commander of the Polish Home Army, gave the order for Operation *Burza* – the signal for Warsaw to begin her uprising.

Fierce fighting

By mid-August, as the Warsaw Uprising was weakening, the Polish 1st Armoured Division was given orders by Montgomery to close the Falaise Gap. Just days before, the Americans had been firmly established in Argentan but Montgomery sent a telegram to Churchill stating that while the circle was almost closed, the Allies were yet to take Falaise. With the British and Canadians straining to get to the Falaise area quickly, the Allied air force set about bombing German targets night and day, based on information sent by Montgomery's intelligence staff that German soldiers were still within the ring and unable to move out due to petrol shortages. With fighting continuing from land and air, and the Americans and Canadians poised to hold their lines firmly and stave off any attack, stubborn enemy resistance continued west of the Falaise and Argentan road. By 17 August, the Allies had captured 140,000 prisoners.

Upon relieving Kluge of his command, FM Model gave the order to attack the Trun-Chambois area on 18 August. The pocket was still open. Two days later, when his subordinates were ready to act on the command, however, both Trun and Chambois were lost. The Americans and Poles now prepared to defend Chambois from the Germans trapped inside the pocket. The only way out for the Germans was to drive the Allies away clear of the two roads to Vimoutiers. This needed to be done speedily and before Allied reinforcements could arrive.

On 18 August, Montgomery confirmed that the Polish Armoured Division had closed the Falaise Gap and had reached Trun and were now pushing further on to Chambois. Still uncertain about what the troops were facing inside the ring, and about the German numbers that had got out to the east, Montgomery was convinced that the Germans would attempt a major breakout. However, air action had inflicted many casualties not only on the enemy but also on the Allies. On 19 August, Montgomery reported to Churchill that: 'The whole area Falaise Vamoutiers Argentan Putanges is a scene of great destruction with burning tanks and M.T. … One column of over 3000 plus was caught head to tail and almost totally destroyed.'

On 21 August, Montgomery confirmed that the 4th and 5th SS Panzer Divisions were still inside the pocket attempting to escape eastwards, as well as German troops outside the pocket counter-attacking westwards towards Chambois in an attempt to help them get out. A corridor therefore remained open for the Germans between St Lambert and Chambois.

The crucial role of closing that escape route fell to the Polish forces. For 48 hours, they took the brunt of incessant German panzer units attacking and attempting to break free. On the same day, positioned on a ridge north-east of Chambois, Hill 262, the Poles commanded a good defensive position. However, finding themselves cut off from all sides by German units attempting to get out of the pocket through the one escape route remaining to them, heavy fighting ensued. With shortages of petrol and ammunition, and encumbered with prisoners and wounded soldiers, the Poles were reliant on the Allies for support if they were to hold their defensive positions. Coming under sustained attack, the Poles managed to do this, holding the ridge until the Canadian Grenadier Guards arrived.

On the evening of 21 August, the commander of the Polish 2nd Armoured Regiment, Col Karol Maresch, described the Germans as 'utterly shattered … the division as having accomplished an extremely hard order, achieving complete success and significantly contributing to the battle.' It has often been acknowledged that Allied artillery was key to the outcome of the Battle of Normandy.

The aftermath

Having received daily telegrams from Montgomery, Churchill was keen to know exact numbers of Germans captured. By 17 August, an estimated 140,000 prisoners had been taken. The last two days of fighting had seen the capture of a further 25,000 men from within the pocket. With 16 German divisions crushed, Churchill had expected the number of prisoners to be in the hundreds of thousands.

On the ground were scenes of complete devastation, the roads littered with corpses and burned-out tanks and vehicles. On 26 August, Montgomery visited the parts of the pocket where the heaviest fighting took place. He later wrote to Churchill: 'I have never before seen such signs of carnage and destruction and the whole area gives a vivid picture of the torment of a defeated army.'

This bloody engagement was the final stage of the Battle of Falaise and the Normandy campaign. A day later, all resistance in Paris ceased and France's capital city was liberated. The Battle of Falaise proved to be a victory of far-reaching consequences, paving the way for the liberation of France, Holland and Belgium and pushing the German forces back towards their own borders, but there is no doubt that the toll inflicted both on the soldiers and the civilian residents of the towns caught up in the fighting was shocking in its extent.

MILITARY ABBREVIATIONS

Adm	Admiral	Lt Col	Lieutenant Colonel
AF	Admiral of the Fleet	Lt Gen	Lieutenant General
Air Chf Mshl	Air Chief Marshal	Maj	Major
Brig	Brigadier	Maj Gen	Major General
Capt	Captain	Mshl	Marshal
Cdr	Commander	MTB	Motor Torpedo Boat
CO	Commanding Officer	PO	Pilot Officer
Col	Colonel	R Adm	Rear Admiral
Cpl	Corporal	RAF	Royal Air Force
Flt Lt	Flight Lieutenant	RM	Royal Marines
Flt Sgt	Flight Sergeant	RN	Royal Navy
FM	Field Marshal	Sgt	Sergeant
Gen	General	SOE	Special Operations Executive
GOC	General Officer Commanding	Sqn Ldr	Squadron Leader
Gp Capt	Group Captain	SSRF	Small Scale Raiding Force
L Sgt	Lance Sergeant	Wg Cdr	Wing Commander
Lt	Lieutenant	WO	Warrant Officer
Lt Cdr	Lieutenant Commander		

INDEX

References to images are in **bold**.